The Spiral Chrysalis

Glynne MacLean

Published by Pearson Education Limited, Edinburgh Gate, Harlow, Essex, CM20 2JE
Registered company number: 872828

www.pearsonschools.co.uk

First published by Pearson Education New Zealand
a division of Pearson New Zealand Ltd
67 Apollo Drive, Rosedale, North Shore 0632, New Zealand
Associated companies throughout the world

Text © Pearson Education New Zealand 2007

Designed by Suzanne Wesley
Illustrated by Katie McCormick and Astrid Matijasevich

The right of Glynne MacLean to be identified as author of this work has been
asserted by her in accordance with the Copyright, Designs and Patents Act 1988.

First published 2007
This edition published 2012

2023
11

British Library Cataloguing in Publication Data
A catalogue record for this book is available from the British Library

ISBN 978-0-43507-614-6

Printed and bound in Great Britain by Ashford Colour Press Ltd.

Acknowledgements
We would like to thank the children and teachers of Bangor Central Integrated
Primary School, NI; Bishop Henderson C of E Primary School, Somerset; Brookside
Community Primary School, Somerset; Cheddington Combined School,
Buckinghamshire; Cofton Primary School, Birmingham; Dair House Independent
School, Buckinghamshire; Deal Parochial School, Kent; Lawthorn Primary School,
North Ayrshire; Newbold Riverside Primary School, Rugby and Windmill Primary
School, Oxford for their invaluable help in the development and trialling of the Bug
Club resources.

Every effort has been made to contact copyright holders of material reproduced in
this book. Any omissions will be rectified in subsequent printings if notice is given
to the publishers.

A division of Pearson New Zealand Ltd

Contents

The Discovery

Nareen Lane climbed as fast as she could until the sound of her parents' shouting was nothing more than a murmur beneath the crackle of cicadas singing in the trees. She couldn't remember the last time her parents had had a normal conversation, let alone been nice to each other.

Other kids' parents got divorced when they didn't get along, but Nareen couldn't count how many times her mother had decreed, "Your father and I are agreed. There is no way our children are going to grow up in a broken home." Neither parent had bothered to ask Nareen or her brothers if living in the crossfire beat a broken home.

At the top of the property, Nareen sat down, leaning her back against the warm wood of the fence. This patch of sunshine between the last of the trees and the Eastern Walkway, snaking along the windswept ridge line, was her private place. Her twin brother, Carl, was too lazy to climb this high. Her mother and baby brother didn't venture up past the clothesline and her father was only interested in the trees, ferns, birds and lizards on their property. Although Nareen often heard snatches of conversation from the walkway, no one ever looked over the fence.

Up here, Nareen felt as if she ruled the world. To the left she could see Lyall Bay, Cook Strait and the peaks of the mountains in the distance. To the right she could see across Evans Bay to the top of Mount Victoria. Below, alive with scurrying ants, was the airport. It was perched on a skinny bit of land so short that Nareen held her breath every time a jet touched down. All around, the hills of Wellington were turning gold. It seemed as if the earth had at last discovered it was spring and ordered the broom to flower. It would only be a few months now before the hills turned scarlet with summer blooms. Then it would be the end of the school year and the start of the summer holidays.

Sweeping her hands through the wealth of long grass beside her, Nareen felt something gnarled and dry catch at her fingers. There, hanging by a tendril, was a chrysalis. Not the usual, narrow, cone-shaped butterfly chrysalis, but a chrysalis curled in a spiral like a half-open spring.

Nareen stared, barely daring to believe her eyes.

Could it be the spiral chrysalis she had been searching for as long as she could remember? She knew that the spiral was the most common shape in nature, but was this the right sort of spiral? Gran had told her that it had to be a sinistral spiral — one that followed the shadows left by the southern hemisphere sun as it traversed the sky. It was years before Gran explained that what she meant was that it had to wind anticlockwise.

Nareen tilted back the blade of grass the chrysalis hung off, swinging it into the sunshine. She wasn't mistaken. It was definitely a chrysalis and, yes, it did spiral from right to left.

She'd found one!

But was the spiral the length of her little finger? If not, it wasn't destined for her and, no matter what she did, she wouldn't be able to open it. Holding her breath Nareen slid down on to her belly and compared the length of her finger to the chrysalis.

They matched.

It was there, waiting for her. The years of looking had paid off. Nareen had once let slip to Carl that she was on the lookout for one. He had taunted her, saying she'd believe anything. And yet here it was, right in front of her, a chrysalis cracked and wrinkled with a million tiny roads like those on Gran's hands.

"Sapphire," murmured Nareen. Gran had said that coiled inside the chrysalis lay a cool, licking fire the colour of sapphire, breathing and alive. A fire cloaked in brown.

You mustn't breathe on it, she'd said, *or it will die. Use the incantation to open it or it will die.* Gran had died . . . whispering of a blue called sapphire. A blue that didn't succumb to clouds or darkness. A blue that burned from within. It had coloured her mind, they said, burned it blue with knowledge of life and time. Knowledge not meant for humans, they'd said, but Gran was human and she had seen. No one disputed that.

And here, less than a year since Gran had died, hung a spiral chrysalis, breathing with unseen fire. Nareen sat transfixed, aware of having a choice and yet magnetically drawn to the incantation printed on her soul. All she had to do was speak the words that would release the sapphire and take her — not one step upon a spiralling staircase, but sweep her far, far beyond to who knows where.

But did she dare?

And, if she did, who would believe her?

Her mother would say it was a "phase" and Carl would trumpet that she'd finally lost it. The only reason people had believed Gran was because she was a schoolteacher. That and the fact that she'd found and opened her chrysalis at a school fair in front of scores of witnesses.

Kelly would know what to do. Her best friend Kelly always had an opinion on everything. Nareen unclipped her mobile from her belt and sent a quick text. Less than ten seconds later, her phone beeped. All the message said was, "werru?"

Nareen thumbed back her answer: "up the back. ruup4it?"

Within a heartbeat Kelly replied, "sus".

It was an hour before Kelly tossed her bag over the walkway fence. She climbed over, rabbiting on about how long it took to get a bus, how steep the hills were around here and why, oh why, couldn't Nareen live on the flat or at the very least at the bottom of the hill? She dropped down beside Nareen. Flicking her fluffy blonde hair out of her eyes, she said, "You'll never believe it. That pesky twin of yours texted me."

"What did he say?" Nareen asked, smothering a giggle.

"Not much. Just hi. I didn't answer and don't you dare tell him I like him. I mean it, Nareen. I'd die if he found out."

Nareen zipped her fingers across her lips. "He won't hear it from me. How embarrassing, you fancying Carl. Ooo!"

"I don't! Anyway, am I up for what?"

Nareen pointed to the chrysalis, watching for any hint of mockery in her friend's expression. Kelly stopped talking for a split second then said very slowly, "Is that what I think it is?"

Nareen nodded.

"And can you . . . I mean . . . do you think it's for you?"

"I think so," Nareen said.

"Well!"

"Well what?"

"Do it. Open it! You do know what to say, don't you?"

Nareen nodded.

"Well, what are you waiting for? Go on."

Nareen took a deep breath, reciting in her mind the incantation her gran had taught her. She opened her mouth to speak, but no sound came out. She shook her head and said, "I can't, Kelly. What if something bad happens?"

Kelly grinned. "You mean what if you end up daft, like your gran?"

"She wasn't daft!"

"No, just ancient," giggled Kelly.

"Say the incantation with me." Nareen saw doubt cloud her friend's bright blue eyes and added, "please".

"But I thought it was a family thing," Kelly said. "You know, just your family. I didn't think it would work for anyone else."

"Then you've nothing to lose. Say it — or not. Either way, you won't be affected."

"Okay," Kelly said, "I'll beat three. After three."

At the third beat of Kelly's finger they began chanting in slow unison, pausing for Kelly's downbeat before starting each new line.

"Fire of sapphire,
stairway of time

hidden and creased
I grant you release
stairway sublime"

In the split second before Kelly's finger dropped for the last line Carl leapt out from behind a tree and bellowed,

"uncoil and unwind."

Nareen sprang to her feet, screaming at Carl, "Get lost!" But before she could shout at him to mind his own business, the ground began to shudder. Kelly grabbed at the fence, hauling Nareen down beside her, as a whirlwind of sapphire blue erupted from the chrysalis and the whole hillside began to quake. Carl, his scruffy hair standing on end, stood agog, frozen like an opossum in headlights as the whirlwind spun towards him.

Kelly shrieked at Carl to run, but her cry was shredded by the howl of the spiralling wind. Through the barrage of flying leaves, sticks and pine needles, Nareen saw fully grown trees begin to pitch and heave like boats on a storm-lashed sea — and still Carl didn't run. He just stood there in horrified awe as the sapphire coil engulfed him and began to squeeze like a boa constrictor. It spun faster and faster, tighter and tighter, hurling more and more debris until Nareen and Kelly were forced to hunker down beside the fence.

In the eerie stillness that followed, Nareen cautiously raised her head. Beside her, Kelly's skin and hair were coated in a fine dusting of soil. There were so many pine needles sticking out of Kelly's T-shirt that she looked like a voodoo doll.

Nareen sat up. Her arms and face were stinging. She dusted off her face and flicked the rubbish out of her ponytail, then turned around.

A deep furrow scoured into the ground marked the path of the whirlwind. Where Carl had stood, there remained just a wisp of sapphire thread, standing completely straight, extending from the ground far up into the sky.

Where's Carl?

"What happened?" asked Kelly, dusting herself off as she sat up. "Was that an earthquake? Look at my T-shirt. What a mess. It took ages to convince Mum to buy it for me. She'll kill me if she sees it like this. Help me pull these out will you? Nareen have you gone deaf or what?"

Nareen shook her head, unable to take her eyes off the pulsating thread of blue light.

"Yuk, these things have got resin on them," Kelly grumbled, intent on extracting pine needles from her shirt. When Nareen still didn't answer, Kelly looked around, the irritation in her face fading. "Hang on a minute. Where's Carl? What's that?" she asked.

Not trusting herself to speak, Nareen staggered to her feet and took two tentative steps towards the spot where Carl had been standing. She had no idea what had happened but she was sure that it had to be bad. Nothing Gran had said suggested that anybody had ever vanished, but then she'd never said it was possible for anyone to interfere as Carl had done. Why couldn't he have just minded his own business? Close up, she could hear the thread humming like a tuning fork. There was no heat coming off it, so Nareen stretched out her hand to touch the sapphire light.

"Come off it, Nareen," Kelly said, grabbing her arm and dragging her down towards the trees. "He's just hiding somewhere. Carl! Where are you? Come on, stop being a pest and come out. It's not funny . . ."

"It's no good, Kelly," Nareen said quietly. "He's gone."

"What do you mean, he's gone?" demanded Kelly. "People don't just vaporise in whirlwinds. Not even in blue whirlwinds. Anyway, I told him to run."

"He didn't, though. He was standing right there. The spiral engulfed him. I saw it squeezing him. He isn't hiding." She was about to say that Carl couldn't have got away when they heard the crackle of footsteps in the undergrowth and the rustle of branches being thrust out of the way. Nareen turned back uphill, brushing the tears from her eyes. Carl would be merciless if he thought he'd made her cry. She'd never hear the end of it. She'd let Kelly tell him off while she got herself together, but all Kelly said was, "Hello, Mr Lane."

"Hello, Kelly. Are you and Nareen okay? It was a big shake. Had to be at least six on the Richter scale." He put his arm round Nareen's shoulders, "Thank God you're all right. Come on. You two are best out of the trees in case there are aftershocks. It's pretty normal after an earthquake that size. There's a bit of a mess in the house. Cupboards emptied and that sort of thing. Your mum and the baby are fine, but Carl's nowhere to be seen. He wasn't up here with you, was he?"

Nareen's father picked up on their exchange of glances and added, "What? Was he up here?"

Kelly began picking pine needles out of her T-shirt again.

"Well?"

"I'm sorry, Dad. We didn't mean to. He just leapt out of the trees and interrupted us. If he'd been minding his own business, nothing would have happened. I'm sure of it. Please don't be angry. It was fine until he interfered and now . . . well . . . now . . . " She trailed off as they cleared the last of the trees, bracing for her father's eruption.

There was none. His mouth dropped open and all colour drained from his face as he stared at the light, murmuring, "No, please no. No. Not again." At last, he dragged his eyes away from the light and, turning to the girls, said very slowly, "There won't be any aftershocks. It wasn't an earthquake. Sit down and tell me exactly what happened. Leave nothing out."

When Nareen had finished he muttered to himself, "A parent's worst nightmare." He put his hand over his mouth, as if he was feeling ill. Finally he asked, "Were you two saying the incantation together?"

Nareen nodded, unnerved by her father's quiet reaction. Usually he'd bellow and deliver a lecture about responsibility in what her mother called his "auditorium voice". Nareen had never seen him look so serious or so old.

Shaking his head, he said quietly, "I don't know how many times I've told you not to mess with things you don't understand. I should never have let you spend all that time with your gran.

And now you have no idea what you've done. Have you?"

Nareen stole a look at Kelly. She had stopped picking at her T-shirt and was staring at her hands.

"Have you?" he asked again. But the anguish on his face showed he already knew the answer.

"No," Nareen said.

"Your brother is trapped somewhere inside that spiral you've released. You've only got a week to get him out. That link," he pointed up at the thread, "will fade away. Once it's gone, there's no way back for Carl."

His eyes went from Nareen to Kelly and back again, a look of helplessness on his face. "Do you understand? No way back. He'll die. And what's worse — I can't help you. I can't fix this. Only those who open a chrysalis can close it. No one else can do it for you. If I, or anyone else, even try to help, it'll vanish and Carl with it."

He got to his feet. "Kelly, I'll ring your mother and tell her you're staying here this week. Nareen, I'll have a look in my study to see if there are any of your gran's papers left in there that might be useful. You've only got a week. One week. So please rack your brains and see if there's anything you remember your gran saying that might help. There's no time to waste."

As he turned to leave, Nareen leapt to her feet. "But Dad . . . " she faltered.

When he looked back for a second, Nareen thought he was going to cry. He exhaled slowly. "No buts, Nareen. You've no idea how much I wish I did know how to fix it. But I don't. I can't help. In the meantime, leave explaining Carl's absence to your mother to me. I don't want you frightening her as well. Get Carl back.

"And don't go blaming your brother," he added over his shoulder. "You're the eldest, you're supposed to be setting an example. He couldn't have interfered if you weren't messing around with that spiral chrysalis in the first place."

"Eldest by all of two minutes," muttered Nareen. "Why does he always throw that one at me? How much more am I supposed to know about life, the universe and everything by living exactly two minutes longer than my brother?"

"That's it!" said Kelly. "You're twins. Don't you two have some sort of psychic connection?"

"No. He's just my brother — and a pesky nuisance at that."

"Think about it, Nareen. You're always reading stuff like that about twins. I mean, don't you feel his pain or sort of know where he is . . . "

"If I knew where he was," retorted Nareen, "I'd never have started saying that incantation with him hiding behind that tree, would I? He's just my brother, okay?"

"No need to get snarky. It was just a thought and, anyway, how could we have opened the chrysalis if it wasn't for him. You know, length of the little finger and all that stuff?"

Nareen shrugged. "I suppose our little fingers must be the same length because we're the same age with the same parents. I don't know. Just don't start about him being my twin, okay?"

She got to her feet and climbed back up to the spot where Carl had been. Her dad had said the thread was a link. Why hadn't Gran warned her? She reached out and touched the line of blue light. It was cold and streamed over her fingers the way water out of a tap does, but that was all. She felt no sense of communication, no bright ideas suddenly occurred to her. It didn't even feel supernatural. In fact, if anything, it felt slightly familiar somehow, as if she'd done this before or at least on some level expected it to feel like that.

Had she? Or had she just seen something like it so long ago that the memory was vague and incomplete? Could Gran have once mentioned light that felt like water? Yelling to Kelly to follow, Nareen took off down the hill, grabbing at the lower branches of the saplings to steady herself as she skated down the steeper slopes.

The girls skirted around Nareen's parents, who were arguing about Kelly coming to stay, and ducked into the bathroom. Waving aside Kelly's questions, Nareen climbed on to a high stool. With a heave, she dislodged the attic hatch, releasing the rope ladder. "Come on, quick," she said, "before they catch us. I'll hold it steady it for you. The light's on a motion sensor so it'll come on as soon as you get up there. Just be careful where you put your feet or you'll go through the ceiling."

Nareen followed Kelly up the ladder, then picked her way across the beams to the far end of the attic and pulled aside a dusty tartan blanket, revealing her gran's old leather suitcase. "Do you think we can get this down through the hatch?" she asked Kelly.

"They got it up here, didn't they?"

With much heaving, giggling and regular breaks to let the billowing dust settle, the girls managed to drag the suitcase to the hatch. They hoisted up the rope ladder and, using it as a makeshift harness, lowered the suitcase, and a substantial deposit of dust and grime, on to the bathroom floor. Nareen grabbed the broom from the laundry cupboard and some clean clothes while Kelly kept watch at the door.

When, back in her room, they finally got the suitcase open, Nareen began rummaging through piles of papers and cards, each tied neatly with interlaced sapphire and scarlet ribbons, until she came to a large satin-bound folder. She unwrapped its cover of crackling cellophane and set out on the bedspread a set of watercolour paintings. The scenes in the pictures varied; there were a variety of landscapes, two seascapes and one showing a busy café. Some were devoid of people and others overflowing with them, yet in every painting there was a fine column of blue light, always a few metres from the empty carcass of a split spiral.

Carl

Carl slowly became aware of a strange, throbbing hum that seemed to vibrate in his bones. Every time he took a breath, his body ached. It was as if he'd been crushed at the bottom of a rugby ruck. Opening his eyes, he could see nothing but an eerie blueness. It was so bright that it made his eyes hurt. Worse still, the colour was constant, no matter which way he looked. Up, down, left and right, it all looked exactly the same. It robbed him of all sense of distance and direction.

Carl tried to stand, but stopped as a vicious pain ripped through his head. For a while he doubled over, telling himself that he wasn't going to throw up. He repeated it over and over to himself until at last the nausea passed. What the heck had happened? One minute he'd been watching those silly girls try and open that chrysalis they'd found.

The next minute, all hell had broken loose. Why hadn't he just left them to it? All he'd wanted to do was show them how daft they were being. He'd been all prepared to fall about laughing when nothing happened. Then, when they got upset, he was going to impress Kelly with his knowledge of the fake supernatural.

Looking about, Carl noticed that he cast no shadow. The blue light seemed to have no source, but he should have a shadow, shouldn't he? Even at midday, when the sun was right overhead, people had a shadow. It was very small, but still a shadow. Raising his hands, he realised with horror that he could see straight through them. He couldn't see anything interesting, like veins flowing with blood or muscles flexing between bones, but straight through. It was as if his entire hand and arm were transparent — as if he wasn't really there.

But, if he wasn't there, then where was he?

Swaying slightly, Carl staggered to his feet. Every instinct screamed at him to run — get out of there as fast as possible. Problem was, he didn't know where *out* was. He had no idea which way to run. That was if he *could* run. He snorted to himself. Even if he were one hundred percent fit, there was no way he, Carl Lane, was going to start running about like a frightened rabbit.

He was smarter than that.

He would do what they do in crime and history television programmes. They reconstructed the past. That was what he'd do. He'd reconstruct what had happened. The last thing he remembered was being engulfed by the spiral whirlwind. He didn't remember being spat out. Could he still be inside it? Could this place be like the eye of the hurricane? If it was the centre of the spiral, then the vibrating hum could be the sound of the outside of the spiral spinning, couldn't it? It would also explain why every direction looked exactly the same.

For a split second, Carl wished he'd paid more attention in science. On second thoughts, they'd never studied chrysalises that spurted out blue whirlwinds or anything useful like how to get out of the middle of one.

Well, he thought with a wry grin, this was another ideal occasion for his answer to everything — "If in doubt, check it out." Time for a shoulder charge, rugby-style, Carl thought. Fishing around in his pockets, he found a printout of the Nürburgring racetrack in Germany and a biro.

He placed the paper down by his foot to mark where he had been standing. Next, Carl picked a direction and added an arrow to the bottom of the printout.

Then, ignoring the objections of his leg and chest muscles, he hurled himself as hard as he could in the direction of the arrow. He'd gone about six steps at speed when he slammed into something more solid than any forward pack he'd ever collided with. He was swept from his feet and flung in a circular motion backwards. With a thud, he landed on his behind, only a hand's span from where he'd left the printout.

Carl sat rubbing his sore shoulder. The question was — was it was worth trying a shoulder charge in the opposite direction? Or was one thumping quite enough? There was no sign of anything solid where he'd been. Every way he looked, the blueness around him appeared the same. Nothing seemed to have changed.

Finally, Carl decided upon a more cautious approach. This time he'd walk six steps in the direction of the arrow. He'd then stop and try to see if he could touch anything.

Six steps away from the printout, Carl could

26

see no change in his surroundings. Everything was just as uniform and just as blue. Assuring himself that nothing was likely to happen, Carl reached out a hand. Nothing. He leaned forward and, just as he was about to take another step, his hand was caught and spun anticlockwise. The force of it knocked him off his feet. It was as if he'd collided with an invisible but incredibly fast spinning turntable.

He returned to the printout and tried the same experiment in the opposite direction. The same thing happened. After trying the two remaining points of the compass with the same results, Carl decided that he'd been knocked off his feet quite enough times for one day. He declared his theory proved. He was stuck inside the whirlwind, or at least, he conceded, that was his best idea to date.

Carl plonked himself down heavily beside the Nürburgring printout and extracted the rest of the contents of his pocket. He had his mobile, earplugs for his mobile, a USB pen drive with his latest downloaded songs on it and a back door key. Nothing particularly useful.

With nothing better to do, Carl flicked idly through his phone menu. Then he launched into a game of Puzzle Snowboard 3d. It took three games for him to beat his previous best score. It took another two to beat his best friend's highest score. Carl punched the air and, without thinking, thumbed Gavin a quick text — "B10U!" — and pressed "send". Without warning, the sapphire about him began to strobe, breaking up into fast, throbbing, vertical strips of lighter and darker blue. For the first time, Carl saw a semblance of form in his surroundings. His theory was right. He was in the centre of a swiftly revolving column. It was about ten metres wide and reached far up above him — as high as he could see. Before Carl could react, the strobing ceased, restoring the constant, impenetrable blue.

Carl pushed "send" again and again the blue strobed. This time, Carl counted how long it lasted. Just over three seconds. Stuffing his belongings back into his pocket, Carl took six smallish steps away from his position in the centre. He took a deep breath and, for the third time, pressed "send" on his mobile. The moment the strobing started, Carl hurled himself at the column wall. Instead of being repelled backwards, he was catapulted out through the column and out beyond the blue.

Tumbling head over heels, Carl turned tail so many times he lost count. But finally he bumped to a stop and lay still. He was sure he must have broken at least every second bone in his body. Unsure if he dared to look around, Carl first checked his limbs. They were all still attached. His fingers still flexed, his feet worked and, yes, his head was definitely still in the right place. With a sinking feeling, Carl realised that, although everything was where it ought to be, he could still see through himself. He was still transparent.

Unable to delay any longer, Carl raised his head and looked about him. To his amazement, he saw nothing but doors. There were hundreds of doors in every direction: tall, ornate doors; short, arched doors; expansive double doors; circular porthole doors; opaque glass doors; shiny metal doors; mosaic doors; fat green doors and even a narrow, livid canary-yellow door. His mind resisted the seemingly endless number and variety. He closed his eyes, sure that so many doors couldn't possibly fit in any space that a person could see. He reopened his eyes. They were all still there. They were all shut and all clearly labelled "This Way Out".

Uncoiled & Unbound

Nareen was rifling through her gran's Scottish diaries in search of something useful when she thought she heard someone whisper, "This way out. This way out." Nareen glanced around at Kelly, sitting cross-legged on the end of the bed. Kelly was engrossed with picking pine needles out of her new T-shirt and, although she was grimacing as she wiped resin off her fingers, her lips weren't moving.

"What are you staring at?" asked Kelly, without looking up. "I can feel you staring at me. What gives? Have I grown another head? If I have, then please, please make it gorgeous so I can get rid of this wonky nose of mine."

"Your nose isn't wonky, Kelly. If you want to see a wonky nose, check out Carl's, but yours definitely isn't."

"Then why are you staring at . . ." She stopped and raised her head, eyes wide. "Who said that? Are you winding me up, Nareen?"

Nareen shook her head, mouthing *not me*, as the whisper sounded around the room, louder and more insistent this time. Nareen felt her skin goosebump as a second, then a third voice joined in whispering, "This way out. This way out. This way out."

She was about to suggest they get out of there when Kelly slapped a hand over her mouth and jabbed frantically at the paintings. In each painting, where there had been a fine column of blue light, there was now a spiralling staircase.

Nareen leapt to her feet and shot out of the room. She was up past the clothesline and heading into the trees when Kelly caught up with her. Kelly grabbed her arm demanding an explanation, but Nareen shook free, intent on getting to the top of the property. If the pictures were right, the incantation had now worked — the stairway had uncoiled and unwound. Did that mean that Carl had somehow managed to escape?

She'd never before really looked forward to seeing Carl, but now all she could think was that she'd give almost anything to let him be up there and okay. She cleared the last of the trees and stopped so suddenly that Kelly slammed into her still demanding to know what was going on.

What Nareen saw was both expected and not expected. Sure enough, the thread of blue light had changed into a spiralling staircase of shimmering sapphire blue, but there was no sign of Carl. As she expected, the staircase spiralled up as far as they could see, disappearing into the clouds. On every step of the staircase, there was a door. No two doors were alike, but each one had an identical sign engraved on it.

"What the . . ." began Kelly, skirting around Nareen. "What do those signs say?"

"*This Way Out*," said Nareen slowly, "but it's not true — not for us anyway. You mustn't open any of them."

"Why not?"

"Because you'll let the ghosts out."

Kelly snorted. "Ghosts! Yeah, right."

"I'm not kidding," retorted Nareen. "Why do you think it's called the 'stairway of time'? Behind those doors is every possible past and every possible future. For us to get in, we have to climb to the top and descend into the centre. Those doors are the way out into *this* time."

Kelly screwed up her nose. "The way into this time? Have you lost it?"

"No, I haven't lost it."

"There's no need to snap . . ." began Kelly, but Nareen cut her off. "Those doors are the way out for the ghosts of every possible future and every possible past. You open one door and you release the ghosts of one timeline. It could be from the past or from the future. It could be one ghost or hundreds of ghosts. There's no way of telling."

Kelly was still rolling her eyes when Nareen turned on her heel and stalked off back towards the house, muttering under her breath, "You can either believe me or not."

Nareen found her father in his study, peering into a microscope, his ears sticking out like a pair of Post-it notes stuck to his sandy hair. Usually he didn't look up when someone came into the room. He just kept working until they made enough fuss to get his attention. Not today. The moment Nareen pulled the door shut behind her he whirled around. "Any progress?" he asked.

When Nareen told him that the stairway had uncoiled and unwound, he murmured that it was a start, but he winced when she said there was still no sign of Carl. She crossed her fingers behind her back and asked if it was okay with him if she and Kelly climbed the stairway after Mum thought they'd gone to bed.

Instead of answering, he got up from his desk and opened the bottom drawer of his slide cabinet. At the very back, behind the array of numbered slides, each bearing an insect fragment stuck like a handprint in the Hollywood Walk of Fame, there was a roll of paper tied with Gran's familiar sapphire and scarlet ribbons. He extracted the roll and told her it was her gran's list and that she would need it. He said that her ancestors in Scotland had started compiling the list centuries ago and that it was vital that they took with them everything on the list that related to here and now.

Nareen took the roll, wondering if that meant they had permission to climb the staircase. She didn't want to ask again, in case he said no. Before she could decide what to do, he spoke again in a low voice, "I don't suppose I've got any choice.

To stand any chance of getting my son back, I have to risk letting my daughter climb that cursed staircase. Promise me you'll be careful."

"I promise."

"Don't take anything for granted and work as a team. It's the only way you'll beat the curse of that blasted spiral." He turned back to his microscope, muttering about how much he wished his Scottish ancestors had never found a chrysalis, let alone worked out how to open one.

Reluctant to give her dad a chance to change his mind, Nareen tiptoed from the room.

Back in Nareen's room, Kelly was yabbering on her cellphone. She turned her back when she saw Nareen.

Okay, ignore me then, Nareen thought. See if I care. She sat down on her bed and untied the ribbons, trying not to listen in to Kelly's conversation. As she began to unroll the crinkled sheaf of paper, a persuasive voice, up by the ceiling, whispered, "Go on, Carl, open the door. Just turn the handle and pull. Open the door. Let us out."

Nareen froze, willing Carl, wherever he was, to do nothing of the sort. Kelly just stuck a hand over her free ear and raised her voice, though she couldn't quite drown out the voice, which continued to coax and beg.

Taking comfort from the knowledge that, as long as the voice begged, the door remained shut, Nareen tried to concentrate on one list. It was the oddest list she'd ever seen. The words were splattered about the page, higgledy-piggledy, upside down, the right way up; some were even written back to front, scattered among what appeared to be a series of unrelated dates. Several sets of letters caught Nareen's eye. Next to 2001 was written, *txtmsg*, and below 2 January 1522, *lliuq* was written apparently backwards. Above Sunday 1938 was the word *xelet*, also apparently backwards, and beside 22 December 1978 was the word *fax*.

"Quill, telex, fax and text message," Nareen murmured. Really? But, then again, why not? The mobile phone was part of their family timeline, after all. She scanned the page and, sure enough, the word *pencil* appeared alongside the year 1822 and *biro* by 1964. It was a timeline of remote communication.

Nareen wanted very much to search for other timelines in the list, but the demands for Carl to open the door were increasing in intensity now. Nareen grabbed her phone and sent a text message to her brother.

DON'T OPEN ANY DOORS!

Doors

DON'T OPEN ANY DOORS!

"Yeah, right," said Carl to himself, deleting the message. "What am I supposed to do? Just sit here in no man's land, waiting for my silly sister to rescue me? I don't think so. I'll open a door if I want to!"

He advanced towards the nearest door — a circular porthole — then stopped. The question was, he thought, which door? They couldn't all go out the same way, for the simple reason that they were all pointing in different directions. Mind you, there was no reason why he had to open only one door. If the first one didn't look like the right way to go, he'd just shut it and open another one.

Carl thought for a moment longer, and decided to pick something that was neither too grand nor too plain. His father was always raving on about the safe middle ground and, for the first time in his life, the "safe" option didn't seem entirely daft. He picked a door covered in a mosaic of shiny green and black chips that formed a pattern of dots, dashes and circles. He strode up to it, turned the handle and yanked the door wide open.

Instead of a stairwell, corridor or pathway out, Carl found himself looking at his own family, including himself, sitting at the dining table eating dinner. Everything — the furniture, their clothes, the wallpaper and even the food on their plates — matched their dinner of the night before. Everything, that is, except his parents' behaviour. Last night they'd had a blazing row about some bill or other, which had resulted in his mother flouncing from the room. Carl couldn't remember if it was the telephone bill or the power bill they'd been arguing about. He'd long ago developed the ability to block his ears from the inside by concentrating on something interesting, such as the centrifugal clutch on a top fuel dragster.

Instead of yelling, his father was holding court, spouting facts and figures about the exoskeleton of the latest bug he'd dissected. More sickening still, each time his father paused for breath, Carl's mother oozed praise, clapping and encouraging the children to clap like a cheerleader. Even the baby clapped and cooed on cue. Nobody noticed the second, eavesdropping Carl.

Carl shut the door muttering, "Pass me a bucket."

Still grimacing in disgust, he marched over to his first choice, the porthole door, and prised open the brass latches. As the giant porthole began to swing open, Carl was swamped by the roar of revving motorbikes.

This is more like it, he thought, as he heaved the door wide open and found himself directly in the path of five revving motocross bikes. The riders punched the air as they released their brakes and accelerated straight at him.

Carl hurled himself out of the way as the bikers soared in a high arch over the lip of the porthole, flinging mud in every direction. By the time he had wiped the mud out of his eyes and got to his feet, the bikers had vanished, as had the door. The only evidence that they'd ever existed was a trail of spattered mud about three metres long that started and finished nowhere in particular.

"Too weird," Carl muttered. "Way too weird."

The question was, should he open another door or not? Given that the alternative was waiting to be rescued, Carl decided to try just one more.

This time he went looking for the most normal-looking door he could find. To his astonishment, it opened up in Nareen's bedroom. Nareen was sitting on the bed poring over some bits of paper and the cool Kelly was, as always, jabbering into her cellphone. Kelly hung up and swung round to say something to Nareen, saw Carl and screamed.

Carl rolled his eyes. "Calm down. It's me. Okay I know I didn't knock, but that was because . . ."

"But, you're transparent," Kelly interrupted. "Look, Nareen, Carl's transparent, isn't he?"

Carl shrugged. "Yeah, that happened in that blue whirlwind thing. Sort of odd, but cool, don't you think?"

Nareen came over and reached towards his arm. Her eyes widened as her hand went straight through. "Can you touch anything?" she asked.

"Of course," Carl said. "I read the text you sent. I couldn't do that if I couldn't hold anything, could I? Anyway, what's wrong with opening doors?"

"I mean, can you touch anything here?" said Nareen. "See if you can take my phone."

Carl reached for it, but his hand went straight through. Nareen and Kelly exchanged glances. Carl hated it when girls did that. Why couldn't they just come out and say whatever it was they had to say?

"So what?" he said. "I'm dead? A ghost? Well, what?"

"I don't know," said Nareen. "Do you remember dying?"

Carl rolled his eyes. "How could I possibly remember dying if I was dead?"

"Well, I don't know," said Nareen, exchanging another glance with Kelly.

"What actually happened to you?" asked Kelly.

"You didn't answer my question, and I asked first. What's wrong with opening doors? I mean, I found you guys, didn't I?"

"That's it," Nareen said. "You're not dead — well, not if you opened a door to find us. You've opened a door into your own time, that's why we can see you. If you'd opened a door into any other time, you'd be invisible to the people inside but you could have let their ghosts out into our time. You didn't, did you? Open any other doors, I mean?"

Carl thought of the motorbike riders who had vanished into thin air and pulled a face. Nareen saw it and slapped her hands on her hips. "You idiot! Why couldn't you just have believed me for once?"

"Relax," said Kelly. "It's not the end of the world and you two fighting isn't going to help anything. Your dad said we had to work together, remember?"

"The voices have stopped," muttered Nareen. "I should have guessed he'd let them out. Idiot."

Carl decided that now was not a good time to point out that no longer hearing voices was probably a good thing. Instead he asked, "What voices?"

"The ones asking to be let out," said Kelly.

"You could hear them, too?"

"Yes," replied Kelly, "and Nareen's right. They have stopped, so please start from the beginning and tell us what happened to you."

"And what you did," added Nareen, glaring at him.

"Okay," said Carl, "but don't have a go at me.

Just listen." He tried to sit on the stool in front of Nareen's dressing table, but fell straight through it. He went straight through the floor, too, and landed on the ground beneath the house with the floor bisecting his chest below his armpits. He had to grin at the look of horror on Kelly's face as he disappeared, then it occurred to him — if he could pass through solid objects, then shouldn't he be able to fly, too? He took an experimental leap into the air and sort of hung there. It felt odd, but sort of cool, so he crossed his legs like a genie and floated up to tell them about the interior of the blue spiral and the place of doors.

Up to Come Down

Nareen listened with only half an ear as Carl showed off. She had to concentrate on the list. He was making everything sound dramatic and fantastic. Kelly was listening wide-eyed. Nareen almost felt sorry for her. She couldn't believe Kelly could be so gullible. Carl was in the middle of describing the ferocious dirt bikers about to run him down when he was drowned out by the revving of motorbikes outside.

Nareen dashed to the window. The sheets and baby clothes were flapping on the clothesline in among her father's lab coats. Carl's bicycle was dumped next to the old claw-footed bath that the water lilies grew in and the spade was still stuck into the fern patch where her father had left it three days ago. There was no sign of any motorbikes, but the noise was deafening. Kelly leaned over her shoulder and bellowed in her ear, "What's going on?"

"No idea," Nareen yelled back. She turned to ask Carl if he could see anything, and was just in time to see him vanish through the wall. He reappeared outside, pointing and yelling at something neither of the girls could see.

As if by magic, deep tyre tracks appeared in wild figure eights around the clothesline. Nareen watched in horror as clods of dirt flew up into the air, splattering the clean clothes. Then, as suddenly as it had started, the revving racket stopped. In the deathly silence that followed, the baby began to wail at the other end of the house.

Kelly smothered a giggle. "Your mum is going to have a fit when she sees that washing!"

"You're not wrong," said Nareen. She grabbed the list and shoved a notebook into Kelly's hands. "The sooner we get out of here the better. There are the things from the list that we need to take with us. You grab the raincoats, scarves and backpacks from the back porch. Then get the Monopoly set from under the television. I'll get the pasta, olive oil, fruit and chocolate from the kitchen and the stuff from the bathroom. Meet me up the back

— one level up from the clothesline. Quick, before Mum comes out to investigate."

The girls met under the cover of the trees and split the provisions into two piles. Carl was wafting about, flitting in and out of the lower branches of the trees, gabbling on about motocross riders. Nareen glanced at Kelly and giggled.

"What?" demanded Carl.

"Nothing," said Nareen.

"Nothing, my foot! What?"

"Well, it's just, you're always going on about Nareen seeing things that no one else can see," said Kelly.

"Nice change," Nareen chimed in.

"This is different," said Carl, crossing his arms and legs like a genie and floating back and forth. "You both heard them and saw the mess they made. Anyway, what's all this junk for?"

"You'll see," said Nareen airily. She didn't dare tell him, or Kelly, that she actually had no idea what any of it was for, except the mobile phones. She supposed that the food was to eat, but why they needed Monopoly or shoe polish was beyond her. She shouldered her pack. "Convenient you won't be able to carry anything, Carl."

"Tragic," agreed Carl.

"Ready?" asked Nareen.

"As I'll ever be," replied Kelly, "but are you sure we shouldn't wait until after dark, as we agreed?"

A shriek from Nareen's mother as she spotted the washing was all the answer any of them needed. They took off as fast as they could, up through the trees. At the foot of the shimmering, sapphire staircase, Kelly grabbed Nareen's arm. "Are you sure about this?"

"What choice have we got?" asked Nareen. "I mean, look at him." She pointed at Carl. "He's transparent. He's let some mad bikers out and you heard what Dad said — we've got less than a week."

"Less than a week to do what?" Carl asked.

"To fix this. And you have to come with us, Carl. Unless you want to stay a ghost, that is!"

She grasped the staircase rail, expecting it to feel like the thread of light, but it wasn't cold. It was warm like a towel rail and, although it felt solid, it wasn't quite still — it vibrated slightly, like a cat purring. Nareen glanced over her shoulder to see if the others were going to follow. Carl was hovering slightly above the ground, his arms folded across his chest, looking stubborn. Kelly was looking from Nareen to Carl and back again, as if she couldn't decide who to side with.

Nareen shook her head in frustration. Kelly was usually the one who wanted to leap in and do things. Somehow Carl's presence seemed to rob her of her power to make decisions. Pretty rich, since it was Carl who got them into this. Why, oh why, did he have to interfere in the first place? Still shaking her head, Nareen began to climb. They could follow or not.

She had climbed just three steps when she heard Carl mutter, "Just my luck. The first time something cool happens to me and, wouldn't you know it, the minute it's useful it shoots through." He kept muttering and mumbling until Nareen turned round to ask him what the problem was and noticed that his hands were grasping the curving handrail. He was still transparent, but he was no longer floating. She nudged Kelly.

Kelly took one look at Carl and dropped her pack on the step between them. "Yours," she said.

As they climbed, Carl and Kelly bickered about who was going to carry the pack and for how long. Nareen tried not to look down through the gap between the handrail and the stairs. Instead she focused on the doors at each step, reading each sign to herself.

She knew they all said the same thing, but she read them anyway. She tried not to think about how high up they were but she couldn't ignore the wind. At ground level, it was barely a breeze, but up here it whistled around them, whipping at their clothes and hair. Worse still, the staircase was starting to sway. Nareen felt like a tiny bird clinging to a windswept tree.

Kelly tapped Nareen on the shoulder. "Hey, stop, please. I need a rest. I need to sit down. I hate stairs."

"We can't stop," said Carl. "We'll freeze. We either have to keep going up or go back down."

"We're not going back down," Nareen snapped. "So don't even think about it."

Kelly ignored them and sat down. She stuck the pack between her feet and began to fish out scarves and raincoats. She had to sit on the coats to stop them from blowing away, but finally managed to put one on. The others followed suit and then after a short rest the trio began to climb again.

Bikers

They'd gone no more than a dozen steps when Carl said, "Don't look now."

Nareen and Kelly both looked. Far, far below, a motorbike was zooming up the spiralling steps towards them.

"Carl's phantom dirt bikers," said Kelly, giving Nareen a nudge.

"Hurry up," Carl barked. "Keep climbing. They're catching us." He switched on his phone's stopwatch and did a quick calculation. The motorbikes were travelling three times as fast as the girls. They'd be caught before they'd climbed another thirty steps. He glanced up ahead. There was still no sign of the top and the steps were only just wide enough for a motorbike. If they got caught, they'd be run over or pushed off the staircase. He had to come up with a way of stopping the bikes or, at the very least, slowing them down. They weren't high enough up for thinner air to affect their engines. He'd have to interfere with their tyre grip.

He caught up with Kelly and Nareen. "Hey! What stuff have you got in those packs?"

Without answering, Kelly dumped the pack back at his feet and rested with her arms propped on her knees, puffing as Carl rummaged about. Beneath his fingers, he felt packets of dried things, plastic tins and pottles of fruit. All useless. Then his hand closed around a large bottle. Liquid! That was a possibility, he thought. He dragged the bottle out of the pack and let go a whoop of delight. It was a litre of olive oil. Just what he needed.

"What are you going to do with that?" Nareen asked.

"I'm going to slow them down," said Carl unscrewing the cap. "You two keep going."

"Don't use it all," said Nareen, sounding just like their mother. "We might need it for something."

"We need it for this," Carl said. "You can't ride a motorbike if it's got no grip."

Carl took careful aim at the third step below

him. He figured that he needed to pour oil across the entire width of the step and let it dribble down from there. Tilting the bottle as it began to pour, he moved his arm slowly across from one handrail to the other. The green oil seemed to fall in slow motion — so slow that, instead of falling in a stream, it broke up into globules in mid-air.

The first blob hit the step and, with a hiss, released a small cloud of greenish steam as if the step were hot. Nah, Carl thought, it couldn't be hot. It had to be some sort of mist, like out of the freezer. He didn't know if that made any sense. He didn't think oil could freeze, but the second blob hit and did the same thing. As did the third globule and the fourth. Within seconds, he was enveloped in a cold, clammy green mist.

Carl took a step backwards up the staircase, but he still couldn't see where he'd poured the oil. Rather than wait any longer, he replaced the cap on the bottle, screwed it on tight, shoved it back into the pack and took off after the girls.

As he caught up, Carl took a look over his shoulder. The bikers were fast approaching. He could see the leader's red and black helmet and the bright yellow of the motorbikes. The sound of the revving engines waxed and waned as the riders circled upwards towards them. Carl couldn't be sure, but he thought the mist generated by the olive oil was clearing.

"What's happening?" asked Kelly, still puffing.

Carl shrugged, trying to look nonchalant. "Just keep climbing."

Kelly ground to a halt. "What? Don't you think it's going to work?"

"I said," growled Carl, "keep climbing. If you stop again, I'll give you the pack to carry."

"Okay, okay."

Carl climbed, listening to the motorbikes drawing nearer and nearer. He wasn't sure if he'd done the right thing by putting the oil down so early. What if it had dribbled down too far and was spread too thinly to work? No, he thought, it was acting all slow and peculiar. That shouldn't be a problem, but then there was that mist stuff. "Too weird," Carl muttered. "Way too weird."

"What?" asked Nareen, stopping two steps above him. As she turned to face him, she clamped a hand across her mouth, her eyes widening with horror.

Carl and Kelly turned around. The green

mist had thinned out, with just a few wisps still colouring the air. But it wasn't the mist or the bikers that Nareen was staring at. The step across which Carl had so carefully poured the oil had vanished.

It and the step below it were gone.

Even the handrails were gone.

All that was left was a gaping hole. They could see straight through, down to the ground.

The next step below that had the middle burned out of it and the ones beneath it had holes burned in them. Everything the oil had touched had evaporated into thin air.

"Good one, Carl," Nareen said softly.

Carl said nothing. He was still trying to stop his mind boggling. All he'd done was pour oil on the steps. He was no science whiz, but he paid attention most of the time during science because he liked doing the experiments. He knew enough to know that there was no way olive oil could make anything solid evaporate. Only things like acid did that, and even his nutty parents wouldn't pour acid on their salad before eating it.

Carl didn't want to admit he was scared, but the more weird this place got, the scarier it became.

What would Kelly think of him now?

She gave him a rueful smile. "Well, at least the bikers can't get us now. You've got to give him credit for that."

"Yeah," said Carl. "You've got to give me credit for that!"

"Fine," said Nareen, "but will you now believe me that this place is paranormal? You cannot assume anything." She turned to resume climbing. "I just hope you can remember which door it was you came out through. If you can't, well . . . don't ask me."

"Look on the bright side," Kelly said to Carl. "At least we don't have to climb so fast."

"Yeah," Carl said. "You two go on. I want to see what happens when those bikers realise the steps have gone." He backed up a step, positioning himself so he was just out of sight of the bikers. He leaned forward around the curving inner wall of the staircase to check their progress. The bikers were still about four twists below the gap.

"Might be a good idea to make sure they can't see us when they get there," he called to Nareen.

Kelly stopped and looked back at him. "What?" she said jokingly. "You think they're carrying personal rocket launchers or something . . ." She trailed off seeing the look on Carl's face.

Carl was saying nothing. But, he thought, for once in her life his sister was right. They couldn't assume anything and that meant they couldn't assume a couple of evaporated steps would stop the bikers. He opened up the pack and checked that the lid of the olive oil bottle was screwed on tight. He took a look around the corner. The lead motorbike was now only two twists below the gap and closing fast.

Carl ducked back out of sight and motioned Kelly to get down. "Here, use this," she whispered, dropping down next to him.

Carl took the tiny hand mirror, but no matter which way he held it, he couldn't see around the corner. Kelly leaned over to adjust it for him, and got it right first time! Usually, needing help from a girl would have made Carl want to puke, but he reassured himself that mirrors were strictly girls' things. Carl avoided mirrors on principle. That way he never needed to comb his hair or tuck his shirt in at the back.

They watched the lead bike zoom around the last twist. Too late, the rider hit the brakes and the bike slewed sideways. Then the front wheel locked up and the back wheel lifted, hurling the rider over the handlebars and down through the gap in the stairs. The riderless bike somersaulted over the missing steps, hit the step above, and fell backwards into the burned-out hole. Tumbling after the rider, its engine roared like an angry giant.

Carl threw a fist in the air, but his shout of triumph died on his lips. Less than halfway down to the ground, the flailing rider and motorbike simply vanished. And now the other pursuing riders, who were rounding the last couple of twists beneath the gap in the stairs, also vanished. It was as if they'd passed through an unseen divider between the world of the stairway and the reality below.

Pass Go

Nareen rubbed her aching legs as she waited for Kelly and Carl to catch up. They were laughing and joking about their victory over the bikers, but Nareen didn't join in. She had a sneaking suspicion that the bikers would be back. Even so, she couldn't help feeling relieved that they hadn't come to any harm.

Kelly dug her in the ribs. "What's up?"

Nareen shook her head and started climbing again. She couldn't tell Kelly that she felt like a trespasser. Gran had always made the spiral stairway sound like a birthright. Like something she was destined to do, but the higher she climbed, the more Nareen became sure that they weren't supposed to be there. It felt like the time they'd crawled under the fence to nick the strawberries from Mrs Collier's garden next door. But they couldn't turn back. They had to keep climbing.

The sky was just starting to turn crimson when they caught sight of something flashing up ahead. Ten minutes later, as fingers of red and gold laced the sky, they rounded the curving stairway and stopped in their tracks. Instead of seeing step after sapphire blue step they were confronted with a gleaming white wall. It rose at right angles to the centre tube of the stairwell, reaching up so high that it vanished in the darkness. Inscribed on it, in gigantic pink neon letters that flashed on and off, was the word *Go*.

"Go?" Kelly asked. "Go where?"

"Through there, I suppose," said Nareen. "But how?"

"Nah, they mean 'Go' as in 'Get lost,'" said Carl, plonking himself down on the step. He leaned down to scratch his ankle. "Hey, this step doesn't have a door in it."

"No, they stopped about a dozen steps ago," Nareen said.

"Why didn't you say?" asked Kelly.

"Because she hasn't the foggiest what it means," replied Carl. "She's guessing, like the rest of us."

"That's rich coming from you," Nareen retorted.

"Remember it was you who got us into this. You who let those bikers out, you who turned yourself into a ghost and you who destroyed any chance we have of going back down this staircase."

"Yeah, yeah, yeah, yeah. Me, me, me," muttered Carl. "Get over it, sis."

"Oh, I'm over it . . ."

"Hey, stop it, you two." Kelly waved her arms between them. "Bickering isn't going to get it sorted. Come on, Carl, Nareen. Think. What's that?" she asked, pointing at a narrow, horizontal slot on the wall about the width of a credit card.

Nareen stared at the wall. Why did Carl have to be such a menace? She'd never met anyone else who could admit they were wrong without taking any responsibility whatsoever. He seemed to think that, if he owned up, everything would just fix itself. Fat chance. She felt her eyes smart and clenched her teeth together. She wasn't going to cry. Kelly was right — they had to think.

She put down her pack and dropped down next to Carl. She was about to suggest that they work through it logically when she saw he was picking his nose. "Gross! How can any of us think with you doing that!"

"Nah," he said, waving his finger at her. "It's high in protein — brain food."

"Only for a brain like yours," giggled Kelly.

"Okay," said Nareen, when they had stopped laughing. "We can't turn back so we have to get through there. We have to get past Go or learn to fly."

Carl rolled his eyes. "Now tell us something we *don't* know."

Nareen shot him such a fierce look that he dropped his head. "Pass Go and get two hundred dollars — I wish," he muttered

"That's it," said Nareen, scrabbling at the catches on her pack.

"That's what?" asked Kelly, as Nareen began burrowing into the pack.

Nareen didn't answer — she could feel clothes, shoe polish and packets of food. She shook her head and shoved her pack at Carl, telling him to swap. He grimaced and passed over his pack. Inside it, Nareen found what she was looking for, lodged hard up against the bottle of olive oil. Rather than pulling the box out, she prised open the lid just far enough to see inside. Taking care not to dislodge the counters or the hotels and houses, Nareen extracted six Monopoly hundred-dollar bills.

She handed two each to Carl and Kelly. They exchanged bemused looks and Carl twirled a finger up next to his ear as Nareen refastened the pack. "Suit yourselves but it's worth a try," she said, clutching her two hundred-dollar bills.

"What is?" asked Kelly.

"Paying two hundred dollars to pass Go," said Nareen, shouldering her pack. Now she fed first one, then the second hundred-dollar bill into the slot beneath the pink neon sign. As the last bill disappeared, Nareen thought she saw the wall in front of her begin to shimmer. She reached out and her hand passed straight through, leaving her arm apparently amputated at the wrist. Then, before she could react, she was grasped in a firm handshake and pulled through the wall.

Nareen found herself in what looked like a bustling, upmarket airport terminal, abuzz with chatter. There were groups of people lounging about and sipping drinks. Buffets full of succulent-looking food split the centre of the room and along the far wall were rows of shops selling designer clothes, perfumes, gifts and books.

Nareen glanced over her shoulder to check that the others had followed but, instead of seeing a translucent wall, she saw wide picture windows looking out on to a spaghetti-like collection of runways, all busy with a dizzying array of aircraft landing, taxiing and taking off.

Realising that her hand was still being shaken, Nareen turned back to face a portly gent with a great twirly moustache wearing a sort of butler's uniform, white gloves and a top hat. He looked as if he had stepped out of English high society during the reign of Queen Victoria. As if on cue, he launched into a great speech of welcome, pointing out the amenities and instructing her to help herself and make the most of her stay. He finished by repeating that, if at any time she needed him, all she had to do was click her fingers and he'd be there. Nareen extracted her hand and murmured her thanks. Before she could ask about Carl and Kelly, the butler vanished. One second he was there, the next he was not.

For a second, Nareen stood dumbstruck. There was no sign of Kelly, Carl or the spiral staircase.

In fact, there was nothing even vaguely blue in colour anywhere. There was every other colour in abundance, but no blue. Even the sky the aircraft were taking off into was a sort of grubby grey. She turned around and spied a small boy carrying a plate full of chips, crumbed nuggets and barbecued sausages. They smelled fabulous.

Hoping like mad that Monopoly money would do, Nareen went over to the counter the boy had come from and asked how much sausages and chips cost. The ginger-haired girl behind the counter grinned. "Doesn't cost a thing," she said. "Just tell me what you want and it's yours."

Her mouth watering, Nareen ordered sausages, chips, nuggets and an awesome-looking dessert overflowing in chocolate. She chose a table close to where she'd arrived and sat down to eat.

What-ology?

The first thing Carl noticed when he arrived at the terminal was the food. He interrupted the butler's welcome, requesting a large helping of every food on offer that wasn't a vegetable or green. The butler clicked his heels and waved his hands around. Within seconds, a procession of waiters appeared carrying plates of sausage rolls, samosas, barbecued chicken wings, deep-fried calamari and pizzas. No matter how much he ate, they kept on arriving, piling up more and more food on the table until at last Carl cried, "Stop! No more."

The waiters bowed and began clearing away the uneaten food while Carl grabbed a bowl of peanuts and a bottle of lemonade and looked about to see what Kelly and Nareen were up to. They were cooing over perfumes and bottles of face gunk in one of the chemist shops. Judging by the number of bags they were carrying, they hadn't wasted any time. At least it meant they weren't going to be bothering him for a while.

He pushed his chair back and rubbed his very full belly. He could burst. He looked around properly for the first time. The place was weird, there was no doubt about that, but at the same time it was sort of familiar. Not that he'd ever been here before, but it was as if he'd been somewhere that served the same purpose.

Carl shook his head. Nah, that didn't make sense. He clicked his fingers and the butler arrived as promised.

"Sir?"

"This place," Carl said. "What is it?"

"This is the departure point," said the butler with a bow.

"To where?"

"To everywhere," replied the butler.

"Everywhere?"

"Yes, everywhere and at any time." The butler pointed to the departure boards and informed Carl that he could go wherever he wanted, whenever he wanted. Once he'd chosen a place and a time, all he had to do was go to the marked gate and catch the flight. It seemed that what Carl had thought were times on the boards were in fact years. The nearest board offered Ormandville in 1975, London in 1512, Nantucket in 1839, Paris in 2095 or Mesopotamia in 1550 BC. He turned back to the butler. "So it's just another version of the room with all the doors?"

"Exactly. I see you are a scholar of topology."

A scholar of what? No one had mistaken Carl for a scholar of any sort before. It sounded quite cool — as if he was brainy like his father. But more interesting than his father. He wasn't going to run around in a white coat peering into microscopes. He'd be a topologist, whatever that was. Carl nodded, trying to look as learned as possible.

"So," he said, "it's not actually hard to get back to the door I went through."

"Indeed," said the butler. "All you have to know is where and when it led to and take the appropriate flight."

Carl grinned. So much for Nareen thinking it was hard. Mind you, it wouldn't do Her High and Mightiness any harm to think it was hard for just a little bit longer.

"Was there anything else?" asked the butler.

"Um." Carl thought for a moment. He was too full to move. "Any chance of television — wide-screen, plasma?"

"And what would you like to watch, sir?"

"Got any motor racing?"

The butler clicked his fingers and a huge screen lowered from a slot in the ceiling. "Manipulate the buttons in the centre of the table to change the channel," said the butler with a bow, then vanished.

It didn't take Carl long to work out that the tabletop remote operated the chair as well as the television. He extended the footrest and dropped the back until he was reclining at just the right angle to watch TV. This was the life, he thought. Everything at his fingertips. Problem was, he was so full he could barely keep his eyes open.

When he awoke, there was a note propped up on the table. "Gone for a spa & facial. CUL."

Carl blinked and stretched. He had no idea how long he'd been asleep and his watch didn't seem to be working. It said it was still a quarter past five, which was the time they'd starting climbing the stairway.

He looked around. Nothing much seemed to have changed. He thought the people were different, but he couldn't be sure as he hadn't paid them much attention. The destinations on the board had changed though. It now offered Chichen Itza in 903, Estonia in 1933, Dusky Sound in 1793, Bangalore in 1539 and Cameroon in 2716. Of those, only Cameroon stood a chance of having an airport — that's if they still had airports in seven hundred years' time. Too hard, Carl thought. He clicked his fingers and the butler reappeared, bowing politely. Carl asked him where he could find the flight to Wellington.

"Ah," said the butler with a frown. "I cannot help you."

"What do you mean?"

"Precisely that. I can't help you."

"But you said . . ."

"I said that, if at any time you need me, all you have to do is click your fingers and I'll be there. I did not say that, if at any time you needed to leave, I would help you." He twirled his moustache. "I've never even heard of that place. Probably doesn't exist. Now if there isn't anything else?"

Carl shook his head and the butler vanished. He then made a systematic search of all the departure boards. Every one offered destinations that started with letters between C and E. He'd had no idea there were so many places in the world beginning with E. Most of them he'd never heard of. For a split second, Carl wondered if maybe the butler was right. Maybe Wellington didn't exist. He told himself not to be daft. The last thing he could afford to do was buy into the weirdness of this place.

He figured that, as long as he recognised things were weird, he'd remain normal.

Where to Next?

Nareen stroked the back of her hand across her cheek. She couldn't believe how soft and silky her skin felt. She turned her face this way and that, trying to see if she could tell by looking in the mirror that she'd had a facial. The therapist had shaped Nareen's eyebrows to make her hazel eyes "pop", whatever that meant. She couldn't really see any difference in her face, but that was probably because she had naturally beautiful skin. That was what the therapist had said, anyway. She hadn't said the same thing about Kelly's skin. Nareen couldn't help but smile, just a little, at that because, with her blonde hair and sparkling blue eyes, Kelly was the prettiest girl in their class.

Nareen refastened her ponytail. "What are we going to do next, Kelly?"

"Not a massage," Kelly said. "I'm sick of lying down. Let's go shopping."

"Again?"

Kelly nodded. "There are another two lanes of shops we haven't even looked in yet."

Nareen glanced down at the array of bags and parcels they'd already accumulated. "Don't worry," said Kelly with a grin. "They have a courtesy lockup where we can leave our shopping. And you know what? All we have to do is show the shop assistants our lockup card and they'll wrap and deliver everything we buy straight to the lockup. We don't even have to carry them out of the shop!"

"But what else do you want to buy, Kelly?"

Kelly adjusted her new jacket and took another look in the mirror. "Don't know yet. It depends what they're selling." She clicked her fingers and the butler appeared. He tilted his head, listening attentively as Kelly instructed him to organise a lockup. Moments later, a stream of porters filed in again. Each porter took a single parcel then filed out. The chief porter, distinguishable by his scarlet waistcoat, returned with a lockup card for each of the girls, clicked his heels and departed.

"See," Kelly said. "Easy, eh? Come on."

Six tops, two dresses and a pair of jeans later, Nareen left Kelly to it. She found Carl talking to a tall, spindly, pimple-faced youth with sandy hair that flopped in his eyes the way their dad's did. Carl introduced him as Stephen, their older brother. Before Nareen could point out that they didn't have an older brother, Carl said she'd been right all along about the stairway of time being a gateway to every possible past and every possible future. Stephen, he said, was their elder brother in a possible future. Now Carl was pointing at the departure boards, rabbiting on about how all they had to do to visit another possible past or future was to "catch" a flight. Stephen peered out from under his hair, nodding encouragement as Carl went on to say that the tricky bit was getting back to the departure lounge. Stephen had explained, he said, waving a hand at him, that, each time someone took a flight to a possible future or past, they dislodged the person that was themselves in that time.

"Dislodge them?" Nareen asked.

"Yes. They get pinged into here," Carl said. "So, for us to go anywhere, we have to make sure that there is one of us already there who can ping us back out . . ."

"Otherwise we're certainly stuck there," Nareen finished.

"Yeah. Stephen's next destination is Omsk in 1799 in time for the new century celebrations. He's already arranged for himself to be pinged back out again. It's just logistics . . . "

So, Nareen thought, I was right — Gran wasn't crazy. She could have gone to all those fabulous-sounding places she'd talked about. Maybe she really had been a maidservant to Catherine the Great of Russia and maybe she had been at the grand opening of Khufu's pyramid at Giza in Egypt. Perhaps she had been to Bamenda City in north-western Cameroon when it became the capital of the world's government in 2716.

Nareen suppressed a chuckle. Her gran had hated Bamenda. She'd said it was unnaturally spotless and tidy, without a trace of rubbish or pollution, and everybody was just too stylish for comfort. Her gran had always lived in an ordered mess and had never bothered to match her clothes. She didn't care if she wore purple, green and orange all at once as long as she was comfortable . . .

Carl blipped her on the head, interrupting her thoughts.

"Don't do that!"

"Then stop wafting off when I'm talking to you," Carl said. "I asked you where you think we should go to next?"

"We have to get you back, remember," said Nareen.

"Yeah, but Stephen says time doesn't pass here, so how about going somewhere, you know, interesting, first," said Carl, bouncing up and down on the spot.

"Like where?"

"Well, I don't know. That was what I was asking you."

Stephen nodded, jutting out his bottom lip just like Dad did. Typical — one brother backed up the other, thought Nareen. She looked at the nearest board. It read Indus in 2010 BC, Halifax in 1710, Greenland in 985, Guadeloupe in 1813 and Irian Jaya in 1090. None really appealed. They didn't sound romantic or heroic, like going to Cuzco in Peru, the capital of the Inca Empire or Samarkand, Agra or Venice. But first things first — they'd have to find someone to ping themselves back before they could go anywhere.

"Don't we have to sort out the logistics first?" she asked. She didn't want to sound too certain in case she'd misunderstood Carl's explanation.

This time Stephen was nodding in agreement with her. Carl pulled a face, then sighed. "Trust you to make it all boring again," he muttered, just loud enough so Nareen would hear.

Stephen stuck out an awkward hand towards Carl. "Well, I ought to get going. It was good meeting you."

Carl shook his hand. "You should come and check out our time in Wellington next time you've got nowhere better to go."

"Ah, sorry. No can do. You can only catch a flight to somewhere where there's already one of you to ping out. As you guys don't have an older brother, I can't come and see you in your time. But good meeting you, eh."

As Stephen shambled off, Nareen had a horrible thought. "Hey, Carl, does that mean you won't be able to get a flight to Wellington because you're not there any more?"

Carl rolled his eyes, muttering about drama queens with too much imagination for their own good. Nareen stuck her hands on her hips and glared at him, daring him to say it louder. When he didn't, she told him to prove her wrong by showing her the flight to Wellington in 2012.

Tyre Tracks

After three full cycles through the alphabet, without Wellington appearing once on any of the destination boards, Carl began to wonder if Nareen had jumped to the right conclusion after all. Perhaps that was what the butler meant when he'd said that Wellington probably didn't exist. It wasn't just that he wasn't in Wellington any more. None of them were. He clicked his fingers and the butler appeared.

"You know what you said about going to Wellington," Carl began, but before he could utter another word the butler vanished.

Carl clicked his fingers and the butler returned, twirling his moustache, one eyebrow raised.

"As I was saying . . ." Carl said.

The butler lifted a commanding finger. "Don't say it."

"Say what?" snapped Carl. "You have no idea what I'm going to say."

"I do not assist with departures and, if you persist in asking about leaving or attempting to procure my assistance to do so, I will withdraw my services entirely." The butler paused, then tilted his head like a schoolteacher to ask, "Is that clear?"

"I just want to know something," Carl said.

"Indeed," replied the butler, "but you see I do not know things. I do not supply information. I provide services for individuals and groups — here and here alone. That is, those who stay — not those who go. In short, young man, I know nothing."

Typical, thought Carl. Trust a grown-up to find a way of worming out of the tough questions. They always think they're fooling us, pretending to know best, when in reality they don't know anything. He couldn't ask Stephen, as he'd left for Omsk the last time destinations starting with O had come round. Blast! Now he had to find Nareen and tell her that she was right. She'd look all smug and knowing.

But there again, Carl thought, if they couldn't fly to Wellington, there was nothing stopping him going somewhere else while they were here. The only question was where?

Where had he always wanted to go?

The Nürburgring.

Monaco on a Formula One weekend.

Where else?

He'd never been interested in history, so he couldn't really think of anywhere else off the top of his head. He didn't want to go anywhere he might have to be a slave or work in a factory or anything like that. He'd quite like to go somewhere modern and fabulous where he was rich and powerful, but a place and a date didn't really tell you if that was going to be the case.

He wandered around the boards, looking only at options in the future. Andorra in 2015 — nah. Algeria — no motor racing there. Alabama 2323 — nah. Brazil — they had a Grand Prix and a bunch of decent drivers, so maybe Brazil.

He drifted around a few more boards and then saw what he was looking for: Bonn — the airport nearest the Nürburgring. Better still, the year was 1968, when Formula One races were still being held on the old circuit.

Carl wasn't sure if Jackie Stewart or Graham

Hill won that year, Lotus or Matra or was it Denny Hulme in a McLaren? No — Denny won at Monza in 1968. Anyway, just to see his favourite Formula One driver race at the Nürburgring in a McLaren had to be so cool. He had no idea what month he'd arrive in Bonn; he just had to hope it would be before the fourth of August and that the Carl he was going to replace would have enough money to go to the race.

Carl bought himself a cabin bag and filled it with drink bottles, bags of crisps and motor racing magazines. He wrote a note to Nareen telling them he was off to the races at the Nürburgring and set off for the departure gate. The steward at the gate took one look at his cabin bag and pointed to a large sign in red letters.

No Luggage Permitted.

Leave all possessions in the canisters provided.

No Luggage Permitted.

NO EXCEPTIONS WILL BE MADE!

Carl stopped. Did he want to go badly enough to leave without food or anything? Yup — he'd get fed on the plane. It'd be all right. He dumped his cabin bag in the canister and wandered up to the steward.

"Empty your pockets please, sir."

"My pockets?"

"You are only permitted to travel with the clothes you are wearing, sir. Nothing else." The steward pointed to the sign again.

Carl's fingers closed around his mobile and USB pen drive in his pocket. He wasn't leaving those behind, no matter what the steward thought. The question was how to sneak them past, or should he try talking them around? He was still considering his options when something bright yellow shot past the corner of his eye.

Pandemonium had broken out on the apron. Baggage carts had been abandoned at odd angles between stalled aircraft and little cars with flashing lights were converging on five motocross bikes that were screaming towards the terminal.

Three of the bikes split off to form a moving cordon, travelling back and forth across the access way connecting the apron to the nearest of the runways. They managed to prevent the security and baggage cars from reaching the two remaining bikes on the runway. Those two were speeding in opposite directions, away from each other, down the runway. As Carl watched, both bikers slammed on their brakes, twisting their bikes around to leave huge black skid marks on the tarmac before opening their throttles and accelerating towards each other. Again and again, they braked, skidded and accelerated while the cordon kept the security personnel at bay.

Carl was so busy cheering on the bikers, catching his breath as they braked and exhaling a whoop as they accelerated, that at first he didn't notice the letters emerging in their skid marks. The riders were grinding out their third letter each when Carl realised that the left-hand rider had etched D and O. The right-hand rider had made an L and a Y.

No longer braking and accelerating with the riders, Carl watched a lower case N being formed while the other rider etched out an F. The riders were almost on top of each other. One rider was skidding out a vertical line while the other hurled towards him on the horizontal as the cordon broke and three security cars, sirens howling, hurtled towards them.

The bikes skidded past each other, forming the intersection of the final letter, and vanished. Two security cars stopped in their tracks. Three others wheeled this way and that in search of their vanished prey. All were too close to the ground to read the message the bikers had left — a message that Carl was sure was meant for him.

D On t F L Y.

Can't Take It with You

After checking every board three times for Wellington, Nareen headed back to tell Carl that her theory was right. They couldn't fly to Wellington because none of them were there. For once in her life, Nareen wasn't looking forward to telling Carl that he was wrong. It would have been so much easier if he'd been right.

Carl wasn't at the table beneath the giant plasma television screen. Nareen was about to go on looking for him when she saw the note propped up against a half-eaten sausage roll. At first she couldn't work out what it was talking about. Races at the Nürburgring? She looked around for a video games lounge, but couldn't see one. She couldn't see any sign of Kelly either. She picked up the pack Carl had left beneath the table and noticed a piece of paper on the floor. It was a printout of a racetrack. At the top, the heading boasted "Germany's Greatest Racetrack — The Nürburgring".

Germany? He can't have gone to Germany. He couldn't be so stupid. Could he?

Nareen thought of the posters of Formula One cars plastered across Carl's bedroom walls and her heart sank. He'd gone to Germany. She'd guarantee that Carl wouldn't have thought to arrange someone to ping him back out again. She either had to follow him or try to find the Carl from Germany that he'd dislodged. But where in Germany was the Nürburgring? In Nuremberg perhaps? No, then it would be called the Nurembergring wouldn't it?

Where was Kelly? Not that Kelly would know either. But she might know what to do.

Seeing the bookshop across the way, Nareen had an idea. She dashed over to the travel section and checked the index in an atlas. It had Nuremberg but not the Nürburgring. Next she tried a German travel guide. Yes — it had the Nürburgring on page one hundred and twelve. Nareen scrabbled to find the right page, hoping there was only one Nürburgring. Sure enough, beneath the heading was a picture of a track identical to the print-out. She scanned down the description until she spotted a *How to Get There* section. She needed to go to Cologne/Bonn airport, fifteen kilometres south-east of Cologne and sixteen kilometres north-east of Bonn.

She had three options. One, go to Cologne. Two, go to Bonn. Or, three, find a German version of Carl. None sounded very appealing. No matter what, Nareen thought, she wasn't going anywhere without talking to Kelly.

She clicked her fingers and asked the butler if he knew where Kelly was. He consulted a PDA and said that Kelly was in the Parisian Perfumery, shop number two thousand, seven hundred and eighty-four. When Nareen asked how to get there, he pressed his touch screen and waved a hand at the floor. A line of pink arrows appeared, snaking off through the shops.

Nareen followed the arrows out of the book-store and past the restaurant, the café and the spa. She was about to head into the maze of boutiques when someone grabbed her from behind. She whirled around to see Carl, puffing and blowing like a steam engine. He doubled over and pointed to the runways. Nareen looked out the windows. Cars with flashing lights and people scurried like ants around huge black lettering on the nearest runway.

D O n t F L Y.

"Don't fly?" murmured Nareen. She turned on him. "Was that a joke then? Telling me you'd gone to the Nürburgring?"

Carl shook his head, still trying to get his breath back. "I was going to. Nearly did . . . but then the bikers did that." He nodded towards the window. "I was about to get on the plane. It can't be a coincidence."

Nareen wanted to ask if Carl thought they could trust the bikers, but she didn't. There was no way she was risking giving Carl any excuse to get on a plane and go anywhere.

"We have to find another way out, Nareen."

She nodded slowly. They did have to find another way out. But how? She hadn't seen any other doors — not even an emergency exit.

"We can't ask the butler," Carl said. He rolled his eyes. "The butler doesn't do departures. He reckons if I ask him again he'll withdraw his services."

"Come on," said Nareen, following the line of pink arrows. "We've got to get Kelly and work out what we're going to do next."

Carl started to chuckle.

"What?"

"She's going to be so hacked off," Carl said.

"How come?"

"Because you can't take it with you. You have to leave everything behind when you leave."

"Everything?"

"That's what they said at the boarding gate. Only what you're standing up in."

"No — that decides it," Nareen said. "Even if we leave everything else behind, we have to take our packs with us. There has to be another way out. Have you seen any emergency exits, Carl? You know, for evacuation in fires and things like that."

But Carl wasn't listening. He was too busy smirking to himself.

"What?" Nareen asked again.

"Just wait till I tell Kelly."

They found Kelly twirling in a front of a full-length mirror, clad in a swirling leather coat with fur collar and cuffs. An array of expensive handbags and shoes lay on the floor around her feet. She smiled at Carl and fluffed up her hair. "What do you think? Sophisticated, eh?"

Carl glanced at Nareen, his smirk broadening.

"Don't you like it?" Kelly asked. "Should I get the magenta or matching leather handbag? What do you think?"

"Suit yourself," Carl said. "You can't keep any of it."

"Yes, I can. I bought it," Kelly said.

"Nah," Carl said.

Kelly sighed and turned to Nareen. "What do you think, Nareen? Feel this fur! It's so soft. Gorgeous isn't it?"

In spite of herself, Nareen reached out and stroked the cuff of Kelly's coat. She was about to agree it was gorgeous but stopped. Beneath the cuff, Kelly's wrist looked odd. Translucent. Nareen grabbed Kelly's arm, pushed up the sleeve and held it up to the light. Sure enough, some of the light shone through. She wasn't as transparent as Carl, but it had begun. Kelly was turning ghost.

"That settles it," Carl said. "We're out of here."

"Hang on," said Kelly. "I'm still shopping."

"Read my lips," Carl said. "It's over. You can't keep anything."

"Kelly," Nareen said, "look at your arm. You're becoming transparent. Here, compare it with mine." She put her arm up against Kelly's. "See! We have to get you out of here before you become like him."

Kelly pulled her arm away, pushing down her sleeve. "I said, I haven't finished shopping." Waving her lockup card at the shop assistant, she announced that she would take everything she was wearing and the crimson handbag. Then, without waiting for an answer, Kelly flounced from the store.

Emergency Exit

"Typical girl," Carl muttered. "I take it she won't be helping us find the emergency exit."

"Don't worry," Nareen said. "Once we've found a way out, the butler can always tell us where she is." She looked around and asked him if he thought they should split up or stick together. Carl didn't want to admit that he'd rather they stuck together so, instead of answering the question, he suggested a perimeter search for an exit. They agreed to start at the centre of the runway windows. To avoid any confusion later, Carl marked their starting point by drawing a blue X on the carpet with his biro. Then he began counting their paces, but gave up at a hundred and six. To keep following the wall, they ducked in and around tables and chairs, ignoring the doors to the departure gates.

Beyond the last of the shops, they met a blank

wall. Well, an almost blank wall. A tatty poster advertising Nugget shoe polish had been tacked up by one corner. Carl looked at it, thinking it was somehow significant, but he couldn't for the life of him think why. He debated saying something to Nareen, but she was already following the wall away from the cafés and crowds in the departure lounge.

On and on they walked, until they again found themselves opposite the advertisement for Nugget shoe polish.

"We've gone round in a loop. Like a crescent street," Nareen said. "I suppose that at least counts out down here." She pointed to the line of shops opposite the runway windows. "How do you reckon we should check around those? They've all got alleyways running back between them . . ." She trailed off, but Carl didn't notice. He was staring at the poster.

"That's really weird," he muttered to himself.

"What is?"

"That poster." He scratched his head. "It's advertising."

"So?" asked Nareen, screwing up her nose.

"Well, look around," Carl said. "Even among

the shops, there's no advertising. No sandwich boards. Even the cafés only have menus. No billboards. Nothing — except this." He crossed to the wall opposite and straightened up the poster. It showed a smiling man in a suit and bowler hat with impossibly shiny shoes and a woman in an apron and bat-wing glasses holding up a tin of Nugget shoe polish. The slogan beneath read *Nugget shoe polish — guaranteed to keep your shoes shining.*

As he let go of the poster, he glimpsed some handwriting on the wall behind it. He lifted it up and saw, written in a fancy, old-fashioned script, the words *Signpost huge hole!*

"*Signpost huge hole*?" said Nareen. "Did you see any holes when you were checking the boards for Wellington?"

Carl shook his head. He knew he was missing something obvious. It was like when you can't remember a word you know. You can almost taste it, but you can't say it. He remembered his mother insisting he put Fernando Alonso's photograph over the "Britney Spears and the snake" poster. Maybe this was the same. Maybe someone didn't want them, or anyone else, to see the handwriting.

Nah, that didn't make sense either.

"Come on," he said to Nareen. "Let's check the other end before we start on the shops." He glanced again at the poster. "We can always come back here if it's important, eh?"

"No, you're right," Nareen said. "There isn't any other advertising. Did you know we've got Nugget shoe polish with us?"

"Why didn't you say? That's it! That's how we get out."

"What is?" Nareen asked.

"The polish. We make an abyss and use it as an emergency exit. You know, like in computer games." Carl put his fingers together, ready to click for the butler, then decided against it. He didn't want to alert him to the fact that he'd seen the handwriting. Back in the seating area, they summoned the butler and he provided a line of pink arrows for Nareen to follow to find Kelly.

They found her in a café, sipping on a fruit drink decorated with miniature umbrellas and swizzle sticks. Her face, arms and hands weren't yet as transparent as Carl's, but they were starting to glow. Carl told Nareen to act normally — talk about girl things with Kelly. He dumped his pack down by the table and went to order them some food while the girls discussed make-up and Kelly's purchases.

Back at the table, when Carl had finished his pizza and chips, he opened the nearest pack and found the plastic tin of Nugget. He flicked the lid off the polish and gouged out a slab of the black polish with one of the table knives. He replaced the lid and slipped the tin into his pocket, then gently kicked Nareen under the table. Her expression didn't change, but she wound one hand around the straps of the other pack.

Dragging his pack behind him, Carl crouched down and, using the slab of polish like chalk, drew a circle around their table. He paused just before he completed the circle to tap his sister's ankle. He waited until Nareen had slipped her arm through Kelly's then, grasping Nareen's pack strap, he closed the circle.

At first he thought nothing was happening, but then he saw a faint ring of black smoke rise from the polish. He had just enough time to yell, "Hang on," before the floor gave way beneath them.

They plunged into total darkness with Kelly's screams reverberating in their ears. Carl tried to hold on to Nareen's pack, but he was falling faster than her. The further he fell, the faster he went, and the fainter the sound of Kelly's hollering became. Carl hurtled down, his eyes streaming and ears popping. He continued to fall, accelerating until he could barely breathe as the air blasted past him.

Down.

Down.

Down.

Carl regained consciousness to feel his skin crawling, as if a million beetles were marching over him. He raised a hand to clear his eyes and nose and heard a myriad of high-pitched screeches as a horde of critters fell off. He could see nothing in the darkness, but he seemed to have landed in a squelchy bog alive with bugs.

He scrambled to his feet, wiping the critters off his face, head, shoulders and arms, and turned slowly on the spot, looking and listening. He could hear nothing beyond the squelching of his shoes and screeching, clicking bugs. He didn't doubt for a minute that, if the girls had landed in this muck, he'd be able to hear them. "That's the problem with emergency exits," he muttered to himself. "They always drop you in the sewers."

He flicked another bunch of bugs off his legs and patted his pockets. He wasn't going to put his sludge-covered hand into his pockets, but at least he knew his stuff was still there. No telling if any of it would work. He turned round a little further and saw what he was looking for — a smudge of light off in the distance. With no better options, he began wading towards the light, consoling himself with the thought that the butler was indeed going to have to signpost the huge hole that had opened up right in the middle of one of his smart cafés. That'd deal to his supercilious airs and graces, Carl thought. He marked the air with his forefinger: Carl one, butler nil.

Banshees Don't Exist — Do They?

Nareen lay still for a few moments to make sure she'd really stopped falling. She opened first one eye, and then both, and looked about without moving. She'd landed in a huge skip on a pile of what looked like old sofa cushions scattered among stacks of rickety furniture and bundles of paper tied with faded pink rope. She sat up, dusting dirt and grime off her clothes. She spotted one of their packs in a broken washing basket; the other had smashed the remains of some very dead pot plants. There was no sign of Kelly or Carl.

Nareen yanked the pack out of the washing basket and checked to see if anything was broken. Everything seemed fine, including the bottle of olive oil. The other pack had a dark stain around its base but closer inspection proved it to be a nasty, sticky grease on the outside. It stank, too.

Gross. She used the ripped cover from one of the cushions to rub the worst of it off then looked for a way out. None was obvious. The sides of the skip were at least twice her height. Worse still, none of the furniture looked strong enough for her to stand on.

She tried yelling for Carl and Kelly, but there was no answer. So she fished out her mobile and thumbed a text "werru?" to Kelly. She could hear Kelly's phone ringing off in the distance. It was definitely Kelly's ring. You couldn't mistake the high, trilling giggle she used.

Kelly replied, asking the same question. Not helpful, Nareen thought, as she texted back, "ruok? im in a skip. can u c it?"

There was no immediate answer, so Nareen thumbed "cbasap" and pushed send. This time, Kelly's phone rang much closer. Nareen belted the side of the skip. "Over here!" she yelled, and seconds later Kelly's scowling face appeared over the side.

"This is the limit. That brother of yours . . . I'm never going to forgive him for this. Just look at my clothes. There's fruit juice over my new jeans and everything else is in the lockup. I'm a real mess and I've got nothing to change into . . ."

"Any chance of helping me out?" Nareen interrupted. "There's nothing in here to climb up on."

For a moment, Kelly's attack ceased. Then she snorted. "He's your brother. I've got a good mind to leave you there."

"And do what, Kelly?"

"Well, I don't know. How am I supposed to know when I don't even know what happened?"

"We took the emergency exit."

"What?" screamed Kelly. "You were in on this? You didn't warn me or help me get anything I bought. What sort of friend are you?"

"Just take a look at yourself," Nareen yelled, too fed up to stay calm any more. "You're turning ghost. You bought into that whole place and, the more you did that, the less chance you had of getting out."

"I didn't want to get out. What don't you get about that?" Kelly bellowed back. "For the first time in my life, I could buy nice things. Not one every six months when I'd saved up for it, but as many as I liked — *now*. You know how long it took for me to save up to buy my mobile. You're supposed to be my friend. *You know* how little money my family has. Why should I have wanted to leave?" She wiped the back of her hand across her eyes.

"Don't cry," Nareen said. "Please don't start to cry. It wasn't real. You couldn't keep any of it."

"I don't care if it wasn't real," said Kelly, with tears running unchecked down her face. "I was being like everyone else for a change. For once I wasn't stuck wearing hand-me-downs with one new T-shirt every six months. I could buy new clothes. My own choice of clothes. Fashionable clothes. You know, like the trendy girls with all the latest stuff at school." She let go of the side of the skip and dropped out of sight, still sniffing. Nareen thought she heard her say, in between sniffs, that of all people Nareen should have been able to understand that.

Nareen sat down on a squab and listened to Kelly's footsteps fade into the distance. She'd known for ages that Mrs Egan, Kelly's mum, earned much less as a cleaner than her dad did at the university. She also knew that Mrs Egan's wages fed and clothed two more kids than her father's did. It just wasn't something she thought about.

But she had to admit Kelly had a point. Short of her becoming something like a rich doctor when she grew up, Kelly might never have the chance to shop like that again.

Nareen fished out her mobile to text that she was sorry, but when she pushed send there was no sound of Kelly's phone ringing. Blast, Nareen thought, she's turned it off. She cupped her hands to her mouth and tried yelling that she was sorry as loud as she could, but there was no response.

Next she tried texting Carl. Her "werru?" was answered with one word, "Dunno." A moment later, he texted again to say he'd landed in the sewers, but wasn't there any more. "Useful, I don't think," muttered Nareen. At least though, she told herself, they were all safe. Separated but safe. The immediate question was how was she going to get herself out of this bin?

She got up and began examining the contents of the skip. She hauled aside anything that looked even slightly sturdy and stopped foraging only when she ran out of energy. The pile wasn't promising. There was a chair missing a leg, some piles of paper that weren't too rotten, a microwave and a heavy drum with half its lid missing.

The drum, which had "205 litres/44 gallons" stamped on its side, looked like the best possibility, but Nareen wasn't sure if the lip would be strong enough to stand on. She wondered if she could put the seat of the broken chair over the hole and stand on that. She was about to try out her theory when she heard a spine-chilling sound.

Nareen froze. She could feel the hair standing up on the back of her arms and neck as she strained to hear anything — anything at all. It was all quiet now, but the cry had gashed the air like a shard of glass.

Nareen wasn't sure what she'd heard. Her first thought was it might have been the howl of a banshee. Nareen hadn't heard one before, but she'd always imagined it would sound like a cross between a mad dog howling and a scream. She bit her lip and listened. Nothing. She told herself that it couldn't be a banshee, as they didn't exist. They were just a Celtic myth. But, if it wasn't a banshee foretelling someone's death, then what was it?

A dog? A scream?

Or — had it been both?

Had something got Kelly? Was that Kelly screaming in pain? Had she been ambushed? Was she dead? No, Nareen told herself. She had to calm down. Stop panicking and think. But think what? She told herself to take a few deep breaths and try to work out how far away the sound had been.

She'd try Kelly's mobile. Yes, that's what she'd do. She fumbled to dial Kelly's number and held the phone up to her ear. The call had gone through. It was ringing. Nareen held the phone at arm's length, trying to hear Kelly's ring tone, but all she could hear was the soft burrp-burrp, burrp-burrp of her own mobile.

The Washerwoman

Carl wheeled around. He hadn't been mistaken. His eyes weren't playing tricks on him and neither were his ears. The hideous wailing was coming from an old woman hunched over the rocks beside the stream.

He had found the underground stream by following the light he'd seen from the sewer. Carl had expected the shallow water to be cold, but it was warm and smelled of minerals. It wasn't as bad as the pong at the geyser park, but it was definitely thermal and ideal for getting the muck and bugs off him. He'd only got out of the water to grab his phone and answer Nareen's text. He'd been minding his own business, looking for eels in the centre of the stream, when he'd first heard the eerie cry.

The old woman was too far upstream for Carl

to work out what she was doing, but she seemed to be dragging something in and out of the water. All Carl could see of her was her green cape and long, straggly grey hair, falling forward like rats' tails over her face.

Carl crept closer, craning his neck to see what she was doing. Now he could see that there was a red stain floating downstream from where she was wailing. Carl took two more steps forward and stopped. On a rock, in mid-stream, was a badly dented, red and black crash helmet. Carl was sure it was the lead motocross rider's helmet. It had a distinctive pattern, similar to Kimi Räikkönen's arrow design, that looked like a bird's claw print. He took another step forward.

Carl blinked to make sure his eyes weren't deceiving him. No, the old woman was washing motorbike leathers in the stream. Why was she doing that? His mother always insisted his father's leather jacket was dry-cleaned. Carl was sure he remembered his mother going on and on about how washing leathers in water was bad for them and how expensive dry-cleaning was and how his father ought to take better care of his clothes or something like that. Mind you, his mother was always going on about things and, when she did, Carl made a point of not listening. One thing he was sure of was that leathers were supposed to be waterproof — weren't they?

The woman raised her head and let rip another ear-splitting wail. Carl shuddered, feeling as if ice cubes had been dropped down his collar, and glanced down to see the red stain swirling around his shins. He gulped. It looked like blood. It *was* blood. The old woman was washing blood off the lead biker's leathers.

Carl squashed the instinct to leap out of the way, reminding himself that he wasn't a wimp. All the same, he didn't want to think about how the biker, who'd warned him not to fly, had come a cropper. It did look as if he'd met a sticky end.

The question was, Carl thought, did he continue upstream past the washerwoman or turn back the way he'd come? Nah, all that lay behind him was the sewer and the sludge. He wasn't going back and, anyway, what could an old woman do? Besides deafen him, that is.

He was about to continue heading upstream when it occurred to him that blood in the water would bring eels out of hiding. Maybe he should stay put and try his luck? Carl's stomach heaved when he remembered that it was a person's blood he'd be using as bait. That settled it, he thought, he was carrying on upstream. No more thinking required.

He got within a few metres of the washerwoman without being noticed. It was only when he slipped on a stone that she lifted her head from her grisly task. She peered about for a moment, as if short-sighted, then fixed her ashen eyes on him.

Carl's attempt at a casual greeting died on his lips. Caught by the force of her deathly stare, he felt the warmth of his blood drain out of him. Even the water round his ankles began to flow cold. It was as if every breath the woman exhaled was laced with icicles. Her haggard face was all sharp angles and hollows — jutting bones and sagging skin. The skin looked as if blood had ceased to flow in it centuries ago. It was the colour of dirty wax. Even her lips were grey. The only hint of red was in her eyes, swollen with weeping.

Carl dragged his eyes down, breaking her stare, and promptly wished he hadn't. Clearly visible in the water beneath the hem of her ragged green skirt were two ancient webbed feet festooned in tiny barnacles. Carl tried to turn and run but lost his footing and overbalanced forward. As he careered towards her, the woman leapt backwards, dropping her washing in the stream. Carl regained his balance and, remembering his manners, retrieved the torn leathers.

"I'm sorry. I didn't mean to scare you," he said as he waded towards the water's edge, holding out the leathers, but the woman remained poised as if to flee.

Moving as slowly as he could, Carl took a step forward. Keeping his eyes well away from those hideous feet, he laid the bloodied garment on the stones before her and stepped back into the water. "I just lost my balance. Honest."

He was about to add that he'd just get on his way when the woman spoke. Her voice sounded creaky and uncertain, as if he was the first person she'd spoken to in a very long time.

"That . . . is . . . hon . . . est. You did . . . lose your bal . . . ance."

Carl nodded and said he'd be on his way, but the woman spoke again. "Your way to where?"

"Um, well, I have to find my sister and her friend then get out of here. You know, go home."

"Yes," said the woman, nodding, "I do know how you get out of here."

"How?" Carl asked.

The woman shuffled her feet, dislodging a pebble that skipped and skidded, landing with a plop in the stream. She nodded as if to herself and then, raising her eyes to his, she told him, "I will answer that and two more questions if you agree to leave my water."

"Agreed," Carl said. "How do we get out of here?"

"You rearrange the letters," the washerwoman replied.

Carl nodded, as knowingly as he could. There was no way he was going to admit to an old woman that he didn't have a clue what she was talking about. He was wondering how he would manage to impress Kelly with an answer he didn't understand when the washerwoman added, "Two more questions. I will answer only two, so don't waste them, young man."

"Um, how can I find my sister and Kelly?"

The woman pointed to a path leading away from the stream. "Follow the path until you pass the second door. The second door will take you outside. Don't go outside. Continue to the third door. Your sister and Kelly are cowering in a skip behind the third door."

"Thanks," Carl said. He really wanted to ask if Kelly thought he was cool, but he wasn't sure if he wanted to let the old woman know that he thought Kelly was cute and asking would be a dead giveaway. He decided to ask something serious instead so he'd look grown-up and mature. He pointed to the leathers the woman was again clutching and asked, "What happened to him?"

The woman stared at him hard. Again, Carl felt the warmth in his body drain away. This time, he made sure not to look either in the woman's eyes or at her feet. Just as he was sure she wasn't going to answer, the washerwoman croaked, "It hasn't happened to her . . . yet."

"Her?" Carl asked. He was sure the bikers had been male. They didn't ride like girls.

The washerwoman raised her head and let rip another blood-curdling wail.

Carl nodded his thanks. He clambered out of the stream and walked away along the path. When he looked back over his shoulder, the woman and the stream were gone.

The Warning of the Banshee

The washerwoman was right. Kelly and Nareen were both cowering in the skip. It had taken only two of the washerwoman's cries to drive Kelly out of hiding and back to her friend. Nareen was still holding her ringing mobile phone when Kelly scrabbled up the side and over the top of the skip. Dumbstruck, Nareen had stared from her phone to Kelly and back again. It was only after she'd hung up and Kelly hit the redial button that they realised she'd dialled the wrong number in her panic.

Their giggles had been cut short by another fearsome wail. They burrowed under a cushion and stayed put until they heard Carl say, "You can come out now. Not that you're well hidden or anything. But it's quite safe. I've dealt with the old woman. All done." He belted on the side of the skip, making them jump.

"Okay," he told them. "Leave it to me. I'll find you something to climb out on."

Now Nareen could hear a puffing and scraping noise on the other side of the skip wall. Outside, Carl had found an old table and was lugging it back towards the skip. He dragged it up on the step beside the bin and, telling them to watch out, tipped it over the edge and into the skip.

Nareen righted the table, jammed it between the wall and the drum and checked that it didn't wobble too badly. Then she climbed up and out.

Seconds later, Kelly joined them. "What do you mean, you dealt with the old woman? What old woman?" she asked, fluffing up her curls.

"The woman wailing. You are not going to believe this," Carl said. "She was washing motorbike leathers in the stream. They were the same leathers the lead biker was wearing on the staircase. And she said something really weird; she said the biker was a girl and that whatever happened to tear up her leathers hadn't happened yet."

Barely listening to Carl's description of the helmet, the washerwoman and the bloody leathers, Nareen murmured into Kelly's ear, "I told you it was a banshee."

"I thought they wore white," Kelly whispered.

"Not the Scottish one," Nareen said. "The Irish one wears white. The Scottish one wears green and has webbed feet." She waved a hand in Carl's face, interrupting his account of his bravery. "Did she have webbed feet?"

"Yeah. So? You don't think that scared me, do you?"

Nareen and Kelly exchanged glances. Nareen was going to ask him if the washerwoman had granted him answers to three questions, then decided not to. If she had, Carl would have been trumpeting his success and brilliance to high heaven and he hadn't mentioned anything about questions or answers.

One thing was clear. The banshee had appeared to warn them of the imminent death of the lead biker. For all its lack of substance, you could die in this place. You didn't just turn ghost if you stayed too long, you could die. But why warn them, Nareen wondered.

She interrupted Carl again to ask the others. "Why would she warn us? Banshees are only supposed to warn you of the death of a family member. Why appear to us?"

Kelly scuffed the toe of her shoe on the ground. Nareen had seen her do that many times. She did it when she didn't want to face up to something. Her next trick was to change the subject. And yes, as predicted, Kelly changed the subject. She looked up and gave Carl a dazzling smile and asked how he'd opened the emergency exit.

She was being so nice about it, it almost made Nareen spit. This was the person who'd given her a hard time for not warning her about their leaving and here she was charming the silly ears off Carl. And she'd set him off again. Only this time he was spouting off about his heroics in seeing the poster and using the shoe polish to escape the departure lounge.

Kelly was nodding and smiling encouragement and he was lapping it up. Finally, Nareen could stand it no longer. "Excuse me," she said, "but it was me who pointed out that we had Nugget shoe polish and it was me that brought the Nugget shoe polish with us, remember?"

"Nugget shoe polish," Kelly murmured, no longer doing her charm routine.

"Yeah," Carl said.

"Nugget shoe polish . . . " Kelly repeated

thoughtfully. "What did you say was written under the poster?"

"*Signpost huge hole*," Nareen and Carl said simultaneously.

"That's cool," Kelly said.

"What is?" Nareen asked.

"It's an anagram, don't you see?" Kelly said. "*Nugget shoe polish* has the same letters in it as *Signpost huge hole*."

"You just rearrange the letters," Carl said.

"Yes, I'll show you." Kelly picked up a stick and wrote *Nugget shoe polish* in the dust and, below it, *Signpost huge hole*. She then crossed off one letter in the top line, followed by the corresponding letter in the phrase below. Soon every letter was marked off in both lines. "See," she said, "it's an anagram."

"But how did you know that?" Carl asked.

"She's not the regional junior Scrabble champ for nothing," Nareen said.

"You're a brainbox?" asked Carl, in dismay.

"No, not a brainbox," Kelly said. "I'm just good at patterns and letters and stuff. That's all."

"I didn't know you were a brainbox," Carl muttered.

"Anyway," Nareen said, "we have to get on. You two are already transparent and one of us has to stay whole, otherwise we'll never get out of here."

Carl was still frowning, but he volunteered the information about the second door leading to the outside without mentioning how he knew. Nareen shook her head. She was sure that they had to stay inside and keep going down. She reminded them that the room of the doors was *inside* the spiral, not outside it. "We had to go up to come down," she said. "So I think we have to keep heading down. What do you two think?"

"S'pose so," muttered Carl, "but which way is down?"

"There's a lift in the corridor behind that door," Kelly said, pointing to a large door with *Fire Escape* emblazoned on it. "I saw it when I was looking for Nareen."

"A lift?" Nareen asked. She hated lifts. They always made her feel like a sardine about to be squished, canned and sold at a supermarket. "You didn't see any stairs, did you? I mean, fire exits usually lead to a stairwell, not a lift."

"So?" Carl asked. "Since when does what is 'usual' apply in this place?"

"We could take a vote," Kelly said.

"Trust a brainbox to come up with an idea like a democratic vote," Carl muttered.

"I'm not a brainbox," Kelly snapped. "I told you that. I'm useless at maths, science and all sorts of stuff. Taking a vote isn't brainy, it's sensible."

Carl pulled a face, mouthing off silently, the way he did when his mother turned her back after telling him off. Nareen put her arm around Kelly and agreed that a vote was sensible. She just hoped that Carl was sufficiently put out to vote against taking the lift.

He was — so the trio set out to look for an alternative way down.

Demo or Cold?

Carl trailed along behind the girls, trying to work out what to do. Kelly had really chucked a spanner in the works. How could he tell her what the washerwoman had said about getting out of here by rearranging letters without letting on that he'd had no idea what it meant? Even when Kelly had crossed off the letters, it wasn't obvious to him that rearranging them was actually going to work until there were only two letters left in each line. How could he tell them without looking like an idiot? Or should he tell them at all? Nareen would have a go at him for not telling them earlier.

Maybe, he thought, juggling the pack on his back into a more comfortable position, he could bide his time and then, at the crucial moment, tell them to rearrange some letters to get out as if it was all his own idea. The question was — what letters should he rearrange? And, even if he had letters to rearrange, could he pull it off? If he couldn't, it might just make things worse. It might even cost them their chance to get out. Nah, it was at least worth a try.

He would never have guessed that Kelly was a Scrabble champion. What a hideous thing to be a champion at. Shuffling letters back and forth. Ugh. No wonder she didn't tell anyone. Maybe it wasn't something worth worrying about. Maybe she was, as she said, just good at patterns. She didn't boast about being a Scrabble champion, so maybe it was something she did to keep her mum quiet. Maybe she wouldn't expect him to be good at Scrabble. Maybe she didn't like the kind of guy who was good at Scrabble.

Carl decided to put the theory to the test. "So, Kelly," he said, as casually as he could, "any cool boys in your Scrabble club?"

Kelly rolled her eyes. "I don't play Scrabble to travel and meet people."

Carl decided that probably meant "no" and felt much better.

It soon became apparent that the lift was the only way out of the storage basement they had ended up in. No matter how many corridors they followed, or how many doors they opened, they kept ending up in front of lifts or back in the rubbish room. Knowing Nareen would never suggest they take a lift anywhere, Carl decided it was time to take charge.

"Okay," he said, "I'm sick of this mouldy-smelling rubbish. We're taking the next lift we come to."

"If it goes down," Kelly said. "The last two only went up."

"Obviously," Carl agreed. Nareen grimaced, but she didn't object.

The next lift only had an up arrow, as did the next one and the next one. The fourth lift, however, had both up and down arrows. Carl punched the down button. "After you," he said, holding his arm across the opening doors.

He followed the girls in and, like Nareen, dumped his pack down between his feet. Kelly pressed the shut door button and then asked, "How far down do we want to go?"

Nareen shrugged, so Carl leaned forward and pressed the bottom button — B5. With a shudder and a graunch loud enough to make Nareen blanch, the lift began to drop. It shuddered and clattered, seeming to take an age to fall what seemed to be just one floor.

When the lift finally juddered to a stop and the doors opened, they found themselves in an old-fashioned wrought-iron lattice cage. It took all of Carl's strength to wrench the rusty, iron gate back. It protested, creaking and scraping against the concrete floor as it folded back. Nareen shot out, elbowing past Carl, the moment the gap was wide enough for her to squeeze through.

Outside, Nareen waited for the others, fanning her face and trying to calm her breathing. Carl suppressed the urge to call her a wimp. Winding her up further wasn't going to help. He dragged out the two packs and looked about. There was nothing to see except blank concrete walls. The glaring fluorescent lights reminded him of school. Carl slung one pack on to his back and gave the other to Kelly.

She screwed up her nose but put it on. "So, where to from here?" she asked.

"There," said Carl, pointing to a doorway behind the lattice cage. When neither girl moved he asked, "Got a better idea?"

The girls were exchanging glances again, so Carl rolled his eyes and left them to it. Why couldn't they just say if they didn't want to do something? Why did they have to get all secretive and girlie? He squeezed through the gap behind the lift cage and, turning his back to use the pack as a battering ram, pushed open the door.

Looking around, he saw an auditorium the size of a football field, with stands towering up all four walls. Instead of a field or playing pitch, the centre of the room was strewn with obstacles made up of ramps, pipes, piles of drums, blocks and narrow metal planks. There was even a two-sided artificial waterfall in the centre of the room. Every obstacle was festooned with sponsors' names and advertising logos.

"Cool," Carl breathed.

"What is it?" Nareen asked.

"An indoor trials stadium," said Carl, grinning like an idiot. He'd always wanted to go to an indoor trial event, but the really cool ones — the world championship events — were all held overseas. This looked like a really tough course. It was a bit weird that the floor beneath the obstacles was entirely black, making it look much further away and more dangerous somehow.

"What's indoor trials?" Kelly asked.

"You know, with motorbikes. The bikers have to get over all these obstacles without touching the ground or losing their balance. They can't put their feet on the ground. You've got to be really strong and a really good rider. That's the waterfall — I've never seen a two-sided one before. That's got to be tough, eh? They start there." He pointed to the pile of Repsol-decorated blocks stacked dangerously one on top of another.

He was about to point out the rest of the course when he noticed the others weren't listening. Kelly was whispering something to Nareen behind her hand. Typical. Finally they end up somewhere truly interesting and the girls don't care.

He dropped his pack on the ground and climbed down the steps to the entrance to the obstacle course. The moment he stepped on to the plate beneath the enormous *Start* sign, the room erupted into great cheering. Carl whirled about. The stands that had been empty a moment ago were full of yelling and cheering fans. A loudspeaker blared out above the din. "Laaadeees and gent-le-men, we have our first competitor."

Carl whirled back to see a man tall enough to be a basketball star from the United States grinning at him like a hyena. He waved from Carl to the crowd and back again, bellowing into his handheld microphone.

"The first competitor of the day, laaadeees and gent-le-men."

He thrust the mike under Carl's nose, asking, "What will it be? A cold run or a demo run to begin with?"

When Carl didn't answer, he repeated the question, gesturing for the crowd to help him out. The crowd responded with an almighty wave of sound. Most seemed to be yelling "cold", but Carl could also hear the occasional "demo".

The compère dragged his finger across his throat and the sound level dropped, leaving just one or two people yelling "cold". He stuck the mike under Carl's nose again. "What will it be?"

Carl managed to say, "C . . . cold, please."

"Aha," bellowed the compère, "we have a brave one here. He's going cold! What do we think of that?" He stuck his mike out towards the crowd, who stamped and yelled, whistling and screaming their approval.

Again the compère drew his finger across his throat and again the crowd quietened. He turned Carl by the shoulders to face the course and pointed to a row of five crash helmets. Carl was sure they hadn't been there before. He blinked. The helmets hadn't disappeared and, yes, the distinctive helmet of the lead biker was among them. It was undamaged.

The compère winked at him, then bellowed into his microphone. "Take your pick. Who will you ride pillion with?"

"Pillion?" asked Carl in horror. "You can't ride pillion on an indoor trials circuit . . ."

"Did you hear that?" hollered the compère to the crowd. "He says it can't be done! He's chickening out!"

The crowd booed and hissed, so Carl pointed at a bronze helmet decorated with spiky white and green geometric designs. At that instant, the lights went out.

Cold  00:00

When the lights came up, Carl was decked out in motorbike leathers. The bronze of the leather was broken by a twisting design of green and white diamonds that snaked up his legs and out across his skinny shoulders. He was holding the chosen helmet under his arm and looking scared.

Kelly grasped Nareen's arm and pointed across the stadium. She started to say something, but a roar from the crowd drowned out her words. A biker, clad in leathers that matched Carl's, zoomed into view on the far side of the stadium. He did a wheelstand beneath the *Finish* sign and the giant clock that read 00:00. The biker performed a few hops, leapt on to the handlebars of his bike and bowed. Somehow, he managed to maintain his balance and resume his normal riding position without touching the ground.

As the compère revved up the crowd, the biker launched himself and his machine at the furthest obstacle. Nareen watched, holding her breath as the biker jumped, pirouetted and balanced his way across the stadium towards Carl. She didn't want to think about Carl having to hold on to the back of that bucking and dancing motorbike. She shot a look across at Carl. His face was ashen and eyes wide as he watched the biker whirling round.

A hideous groan from the crowd dragged Nareen's attention back to the biker and she was just in time to see him tumble off the top of a Suzuki-emblazoned tower. He and his bike fell at a sickening speed towards the floor but, instead of hitting the ground, they continued to fall. Nareen watched in horror as the biker and bike became smaller and smaller as they fell further and further away. What Nareen had thought was the floor was nothing more solid than an abyss.

The compère turned to the crowds and raised his arms, shaking his head. In the deathly silence that followed, he turned to Carl. "Pick again."

Nareen watched Carl point a shaking finger at a purple helmet decorated with a gold dragon breathing fire.

Again the lights went out.

And again, when they came up, Carl was in bike leathers to match his helmet.

The crowd quietened in expectation, but the hush lasted just a few seconds before erupting into loud cheers as a new biker did a wheelstand as he entered the stadium.

Instead of tackling the course backwards to get to the start line, this one dismounted, took a bow and indicated to a sideline marshal to take his bike. Ignoring the boos and heckles from the crowd, he followed the sideline marshal up on to a walkway running the length of the arena.

Nareen relaxed then tensed again as she realised that this meant Carl would have no choice but to ride pillion this time. She jumped when someone tapped her on the shoulder. It was a marshal. He gestured for her and Kelly to step down into the stadium proper and take two of the spare seats behind where Carl stood.

By the time they were seated, the purple-clad biker had reached the compère. He removed his helmet. To Nareen's amazement, the biker was a girl with fluffy blonde hair like Kelly's. When she greeted the crowd, her voice even sounded like

Kelly's. She thanked the fans for their support and the opportunity to appear again in their magnificent stadium then turned to Carl. "Ready?" she said.

Carl managed to nod. The compère responded by bellowing, "Helmets on."

To much stamping and clapping from the crowd, Carl and the biker donned their helmets. Another marshal stepped forward to help hold the motorbike. The noise grew louder as Carl clambered on to the back of the bike and grasped the bar that formed the low backrest of the pillion. The marshal pointed to the footrests he was to use. Carl nodded and adjusted his position. Even though Nareen knew he stood no chance of hearing her, she cupped her hands around her mouth and screamed, "Hold on tight, Carl. Don't be a hero. Just hang on."

The biker gave a last wave to the crowd, then climbed on to her bike. At her nod, the marshals stepped away from the machine. Then, with an almighty revving of the engine, she crossed the start line with Carl wobbling about on the back.

Nareen wanted to close her eyes and not look, but she couldn't. No matter how hard she tried, she couldn't take her eyes off her brother. He looked insecure at best. The biker started with a wide sweep of the obstacle course, building up speed. As she straightened the bike and accelerated towards the curved launching block, the compère began his commentary.

"She's chosen to start with the Vodafone High Jump — that'll rattle our competitor's teeth a little. What do we say to him?"

The crowd roared, "Hang on tight!"

Kelly grabbed Nareen's arm as the bike sailed up into the air. It easily cleared the bar between two red and white columns and seemed to hang in the air for an eternity. As the bike began to fall, the rider adjusted her centre of gravity. For a sickening moment, Nareen thought the biker had misjudged, that she'd gone too far forward and the bike was going to miss the red landing ramp. But no. They hit the ramp about two-thirds of the way down. The bike slewed but, with an almighty heave, the rider hauled it back on to an even keel.

"Laaadeees and gent-le-men," the compère yelled, "easy clearance and safe landing. What do we say?"

"Next!" roared the crowd.

"You heard them," said the compère with a hyena-like grin. "They want the next obstacle. What'll she choose this time? Will it be the Repsol Pile, the Honda Pipes or the dreaded Suzuki Tower? And will our competitor manage to hang on?"

The biker acknowledged the crowd with a wave and then motioned to an aide dressed in matching team leathers and helmet. The aide positioned himself in front of a collection of enormous yellow pipes propped up against each other.

"It's the Honda Pipes," announced the compère, his voice rising in excitement. "The steepest of the pipes is angled at a gradient of one in three, laaadeees and gent-le-men. That's the quickest and toughest way through this obstacle. The only alternative is to take the easy but long way and risk incurring TIME PENALTIES."

Time penalties, Nareen thought. As if just surviving the course wasn't hard enough. She stole a look at Kelly. Kelly was still clutching Nareen's arm. Her other hand was clamped over her mouth as she watched the aide wave the biker towards the steepest of the three pipes. As if unaware of what was about to happen next, Carl let go a hand to wipe his visor.

"Hang on, Carl," Kelly and Nareen yelled in unison. The compère took up their cry, waving the audience to join in until the entire stadium was reverberating with the words, "Hang on, Carl."

02:55

Pipes & Waterfalls

Carl managed to grab the bar behind his back just before the biker began a series of hops. With each hop, Carl bounced and wobbled. Nareen held her breath as the biker launched her machine from the floor up on to the back of the pipe. Following her aide's instructions, she inched it forward, balancing the bike on the curved surface as she positioned it for the jump to the next pipe. To make the jump, she had to go up, clear the lip of the pipe, and then down on to the lower pipe — all without slipping off the surface. She revved the bike to clear the lip and hesitated. The entire crowd inhaled as the bike juddered slightly. Then, as if having gathered enough courage, the biker hauled the front forks upwards and shot forward.

The bike leapt, then dropped immediately.

The moment they hit the surface of the lower pipe, the rider bounced the bike up and down, almost on the spot. Carl swayed, unable to stay upright. He listed to the left and, for a hideous moment, Nareen thought he was going to tip the bike right over. Instinctively, the rider counterbalanced by leaning her weight over to the right. She managed to hold the bike upright, but Carl was still struggling to right himself. Nareen couldn't bear to watch. If Carl came up too quickly and the rider didn't compensate, they were done for. The crowd exhaled in relief and Nareen opened her eyes again.

Both rider and Carl were sitting upright, but now they had to leap up on to the final pipe in the pile. It was propped on top of the end of the pipe they were on and sloped downwards back to the narrow pathway of floor between obstacles. The rider revved and launched the bike forward so fast that the compère whooped and cheered, winding up the crowd. The rider hauled the bike into the air and skated down the final pipe, twisting her bike to a tyre-screaming stop on the floor.

"Laaadeees and gent-le-men," the compère yelled, "that's how to make the hard and fast way look easy. What do we say now?"

"Next!" roared the crowd.

"I can't hear you!" bellowed the compère, placing his free hand behind his ear. "What do we say?"

"Next! Next! Next!" roared the crowd.

"What'll it be this time?" asked the compère. "The Repsol Pile? The Suzuki Tower? Or is she game enough, brave enough and skilled enough to take on the Waterfall? What do we say?"

"Waterfall. Waterfall. Waterfall," responded the crowd. The chant rolled around the stadium like thunder. Kelly said something in Nareen's ear, but the racket drowned it out.

As if oblivious to the crowd, the biker was doing circuits between the obstacles, gathering speed with each circuit.

"Gathering too much speed for the Waterfall, laaadeees and gent-le-men," drawled the compère. He shrugged as the crowd booed and hissed. Then, turning the microphone up even louder to holler over them, he roared, "It's the Repsol Pile!"

Sure enough, the aide was waving the rider on towards two huge blocks, the size of shipping containers, propped up facing each other across a gap of what looked to Nareen like at least ten metres. Unlike jump ramps, the two blocks were at different slopes and different angles. Somehow, the biker was going to have to change direction in mid-air.

Nareen looked at Kelly and they both cupped their hands around their mouths, yelling as loud as they could, "Hang on tight, Carl."

He seemed to be getting the hang of it. As the rider leaned low and forward over her handlebars, Carl seemed to lean forward, too. But, instead of hurtling up the centre of the first block, the rider sped up in an arc so that, when she launched into the air, she was turning towards the other container. But would it be enough? The aide, standing in the gap between the containers, was waving his arms around furiously, attempting to signal something. The biker leaned far over towards the container they were aiming for. Carl was caught unprepared by the bike tilting beneath him and lost his grip on the back of the pillion. His left hand flew up into the air and the crowd screamed, "Hang on, Carl."

Carl seemed unable to react. Like a bucking bronco rodeo rider, he sailed down towards the landing block with one raised hand scrabbling at the air above his head. They hit the very edge of the block and the rider hauled the bike around, trying to keep the tyres in contact with the container. Carl wasn't helping matters as he flailed at the air, swinging from one side to the other like a Slinky. Just as the back tyre touched down, the biker reached back and knocked Carl's arm down. It seemed to snap him back to his senses and he grabbed the bar behind him as the bike flew down the block.

This time, the crowd didn't need the compère to tell them the rider had done a good job. They whistled and cheered, stamped and clapped. The compère conducted them as if in front of an orchestra. "Looks like our competitor is getting the jitters, laaadeees and gent-le-men. What do we say?"

"Waterfall!" bellowed the crowd as one.

"A little louder," suggested the compère.

"Waterfall. Do the Waterfall!" screamed the crowd, so loud that Nareen's ears hurt.

Sure enough, the aide was scaling the lower part of the artificial waterfall. The surface was so slippery that he had to grasp the wet boulder formations jutting out of the steep, sloping ramp just to keep his footing. The shallow water was running fast enough to throw up spray between the larger boulders. It cascaded down over the smaller rocks and the uneven surface, dropping into a gutter-like vent at the base of the waterfall.

The aide seemed to be verifying the best route. As he did so, the compère was counting down how much time they had left to make it to the top. It started by being five minutes and ten seconds, but the aide seemed unconcerned. Nareen wondered if perhaps he couldn't hear the compère or the crowd through his helmet. But, even if he couldn't, he had to be able to see the huge clock ticking down the seconds above the *Finish* sign. Once satisfied, the aide made a series of hand signals to the rider, then positioned himself on a medium-sized boulder near the bottom and waved them on to commence the climb.

"Heeeeeere we go," roared the compère. "With two minutes, fifty-five seconds to get to the top."

Thumbs Up or Thumbs Down?

Carl could hear the compère and the crowd through his helmet. He couldn't see the waterfall, but he knew that all he had to do was hang on for another two minutes and fifty-five seconds. He was hanging on so tight, his hands felt numb and he could barely feel the bar between his fingers. The bike leapt forward and he started counting aloud to himself, "Fifty-four, fifty-three, fifty . . . argh . . ."

Carl's visor caught a blast of water, and it took all of his strength to resist the instinct to free his hands and clear his vision. He could hear water roaring and splashing, and the tyres squealing in protest at the lack of grip. The leathers above his boots were starting to stick to his legs.

The bike surged forward, then hopped and bounced and hopped. Carl couldn't see his rider any more so he had no chance of copying her movements to try to stay upright. He'd lost count of how much time had passed and had no idea how much longer he had to stay on this bucking bronco. Still, it had to be around two minutes or less, he thought.

He was about to start counting again from the two-minute mark when the squealing tyres slipped and lost all traction. The bike started to slide sideways. Carl tried to lean in the opposite direction, but it didn't seem to help. They were sliding down the waterfall. He could hear the crowd baying for blood and the compère saying they were done for, when suddenly the back tyre hit a boulder. It jammed the wheel into a rut, stopping the back wheel dead. The engine screamed, but it was just what the rider needed. She cut the throttle and straightened the bike up. Equilibrium regained, she bounced it out of the rut and headed back up the waterfall.

Carl unclenched his teeth. He had to give it to her — this girl was tough. Tougher than any girl he'd ever met. Before he could begin to wonder if she was too tough, the bike catapulted forward, almost throwing Carl from his perch. He heard the compère say they had thrown caution to the wind and were taking the hard and fast route up. The crowd stamped and hollered. Carl hung on for grim death. Every bone in his body seemed to be being ground together and flung apart as the bike lurched, jumped and hurled its way up the waterfall.

Just as he was sure he couldn't take any more and didn't care if he failed, he felt the engine cut out. He saw the rider's feet touch down on the ground. They'd either failed or they were at the top.

The biker's aide was prising Carl's fingers off the pillion backrest. He helped Carl off the bike and flicked up his visor. Carl saw the aide's lips moving, but the crowd noise drowned out his words. What Carl did notice was that the aide was smiling, and so was the Kelly lookalike rider.

Carl hauled off his helmet and looked around. They were at the top of the waterfall and the stop watch had stopped at 00:03. They'd made it with three seconds to spare. The crowd was cheering and stamping, hurling streamers and clapping. It was the greatest thing Carl had ever experienced. Everyone was cheering him. Everyone thought he was brave. He was undoubtedly a hero. He took a bow and the crowd went deathly quiet.

Carl shot a look at the rider and her aide, but neither would meet his eye. They both looked at their feet. They stood with their helmets tucked under their arms as if waiting for the playing of the national anthem. The stadium was so quiet that, when Carl shuffled his feet, the squeaking of the soles of his boots reverberated off the ceiling and walls.

A movement high above the start line caught his eye. An opaque screen he'd taken to be part of the wall was rising. And still no one in the stadium spoke. After the racket and excitement, the silence buzzed in Carl's ears. It was one of those moments that usually made him want to jump out at someone and yell "Boo", but not this time. This time it was too quiet, too unnerving. Trying to keep his head bowed like the others, Carl managed to look up through the top of his eyes to see what was being revealed from behind the screen.

Flanking an enormous, ornate throne was a

pair of dozing Komodo dragons. Not impressed, Carl thought, they're just really large lizards with bad breath. That said, he couldn't help feeling just a little relieved that they were each wearing a collar and a leash. From within the shadowy depths of the throne, a small, high-pitched voice said in a peevish tone, "Where are the others?"

"Laaadeees and gent-le-men, the OTHERS," the compère said, waving frantically for Kelly and Nareen to step forward.

Someone in the crowd cheered and was hushed into silence. As the girls joined the compère, Carl noticed that Nareen's skin had started to glow. She wasn't as transparent as Kelly, and nowhere near as transparent as he was, but it had started. She, too, was turning ghost.

To Carl's horror, the compère was pointing to the row of four remaining helmets. Nareen wouldn't stand a chance of holding on. She couldn't even balance properly on a bicycle. He had no idea if Kelly could. His heart sank as the compère said, "Take your pick. Which helmet will it be?"

Nareen pointed to the distinctive helmet of the lead biker, but Kelly knocked her hand away hissing, "Not that one."

"Why not?" Nareen asked, her whisper echoing off the ceiling. "Why not? Why not?"

"The banshee," hissed Kelly. "The warning!"

"Come, come," said the compère, sounding just a trifle stressed, "we can't keep the Generalissimo waiting." He lowered his voice. "It won't do Carl any favours," he murmured.

"She will have that one and I will have this one," said Kelly in an authoritative voice. She stepped forward and picked up the other two helmets, leaving the lead rider's one behind. She handed one to Nareen and placed the other under her arm.

Nareen glared at her, but said nothing as the marshals led them up an access way to the top of the waterfall. They joined Carl, the rider and her aide at the top. Kelly nudged Carl in the ribs and crossed her fingers. He thought he saw the rider pass Nareen a note behind her back, but he couldn't be sure.

The compère allowed the expectant silence to magnify before bellowing into his microphone, "What'll it be, laaadeees and gent-le-men? — thumbs up or thumbs down?"

Part of the crowd roared "up", attempting to

drown out those yelling "down". Carl thought more were yelling "up" than "down", but there was so much reverberation off the walls that he couldn't be sure. He saw Kelly and Nareen exchange wide-eyed glances. Neither looked at him.

The compère drew his finger across his throat and again the crowd quietened. He bowed in the direction of the throne. "The Generalissimo will decide if our competitor has done enough. If he has, it's safe passage out for him and his friends. If not . . ." he paused, waving a spiralling finger down towards the abyss. "Then it will be up to the others. They will have to compete to earn their safe passage out." He lowered his voice and bowed his head. "It is the Generalissimo's decision and his alone." The compère then raised his hands and, darting his eyes back and forth, announced in a booming bellow, "Thumbs up — they live and leave — or thumbs down — he dies."

There was no answer. Carl clutched his hands together behind his back, not knowing what to think. He couldn't shut the image of the first biker tumbling into the abyss out of his mind. It was looping over and over again.

A movement high above them interrupted the

replaying vision. Carl held his breath, waiting for the Generalissimo to appear. From within the shadows of the throne, a small boy stood up. He was much smaller than Carl. From this distance, Carl thought he couldn't be more than six or seven years old. Carl tried to peer past him to see the Generalissimo, but no one else appeared. The boy stepped up to the front of the throne. He stood with one hand on his hip and stared imperiously out across the stadium. Like a reverse Mexican wave, the crowd bowed their heads as his gaze passed over them.

Unable to believe the crowd's reaction, Carl shook his head. No way. His fate was going to be decided by a kid dressed up to look like a general? Nah, Carl thought. No chance. This had to be a joke. The crowd were just winding him up again. It was another test. He was about to start laughing when Nareen stamped on his foot. He winced, and only just managed to swallow a yowl of protest.

The Generalissimo stuck out a clenched fist. The crowd took in and held an expectant breath, but the fist stayed clenched.

"Up or down?" the compère asked him in an exaggerated stage whisper.

The Generalissimo looked straight at Carl. The chill in those pale blue eyes was older than the oldest adult Carl had ever met. He clenched his clammy hands. He felt as if those eyes could see his entire life: every boast, every mistake and every bad thing he'd ever done or wanted to do. Weirder still, the face was an older version of Carl's eighteen-month-old brother. Carl gulped but held the gaze.

With the slightest of nods, the Generalissimo rotated his fist and extended his thumb . . . upwards.

The Letters

The crowd went so berserk that even the compère's "Laaadeees and gent-le-men" was drowned out. The Kelly lookalike rider smiled and waved to the crowd, motioned to her aide and then donned her helmet. With the aide riding pillion, she sped down the waterfall and out over the finish line.

Nareen felt so relieved, it didn't even bother her that Carl was doing multiple bows, each more flowery than the last. She gave Kelly a hug then remembered the note the rider had pushed into her hand behind her back. Nareen unclenched her hand just enough to enable her to read it. It read, *You've changed our lives twice now. Please do it once more. Don't leave us stranded here.* Before Nareen could try and work out what it meant, Kelly said in her ear, "Look."

She pointed to the compère. He was on his way

up to the top of the waterfall. A string of marshals trailed along in his wake. Each marshal carried an ornate orange cushion edged with gold tassels. The closer to the top he got, the louder the crowd cheered. Every time Nareen thought they couldn't possibly make any more noise, they turned up the volume. At the top, the compère joined Carl in a competition to see who could do the floweriest bow, until at last he shrugged and conceded the competition to Carl.

Great, thought Nareen, encourage him, why don't you! That's all we need. Kelly rolled her eyes at Nareen, but kept beaming at Carl. As relieved as she was, Nareen wasn't sure she'd be able to cope with Carl the hero for very long. Finally, the compère gestured for the crowd to be silent. It took three throat-slitting motions before they quietened down completely.

The compère raised his microphone and the entire crowd yelled, "Laaadeees and gent-le-men." He raised his hands in mock defeat, as if to say, what can I do? He waited for the crowd to hush then said, very quietly, "Laaadeees and gent-le-men." Then he bellowed, "I give you Carl!" Before Carl could launch into yet another series of bows, the compère grasped his hand and shook it vigorously. As the crowd continued to cheer, the lead marshal stepped forward to hand a large shield to the compère. He then motioned for the line of junior marshals to step forward. From each of their cushions, he took a word and stuck it to the shield. When the job was done, the marshals filed out.

The compère pulled Carl forward, presented him with the shield then paused for photographs. Nareen caught Kelly's eye and pointed her finger towards her open mouth, but Kelly just smiled, clapping along with the rest of the crowd.

At last the compère ceased shaking Carl's hand, dismissed the horde of photographers and pointed to the exit beneath the *Finish* sign. When Carl didn't move, he took him by the shoulders and gave him a shove. Carl tucked the shield under his arm and, still waving and bowing to the crowd, led the girls out of the stadium. The moment he stepped on to the plate beneath the *Finish* sign, the room went deathly quiet. The crowd, the compère and the marshals had all vanished. The arena was as quiet and deserted as it had been when they arrived.

For a moment, Carl hesitated, as if unsure whether to leave or stay. "Come on," urged Nareen, "let's get out of here while we still can." When Carl made no move to leave, she added, "You don't seriously want to ride that course again, do you?"

"Nareen's right," Kelly said. "You were really brave up there, but none of us wants to go through that again. Quit while you're ahead."

Watching Carl wilt, Nareen almost felt sorry for him. It was as if without the cheering crowd he'd lost a couple of centimetres in height. The trio filed out of the stadium with Carl bringing up the rear.

They nearly tripped over their packs on the other side of the door. As the girls shouldered the packs, Nareen thought she heard the door into the stadium lock behind them, but she couldn't be sure. Kelly didn't seem to have heard it. Carl was looking miserable, leaning up against the undecorated concrete wall of the corridor.

To make him feel better, she asked, "What does the shield say?"

Carl fished it out from under his arm and turned it the right way up. He pulled a face and stuck it back under his arm.

"Well?" asked Kelly.

"Just garbage," Carl muttered. At Kelly's insistence, he handed her the shield. With Nareen peering over her shoulder, she read, *An energetic world leader remains*. What does that mean?"

"I told you," snapped Carl. "It's garbage."

Nareen tapped Kelly on the shoulder. "That reminds me. What was all that stuff about the helmet I picked?"

"The banshee, remember?" Kelly said.

"I got that it was about the banshee," Nareen said, "but what *about* the banshee?"

"That was the lead biker's helmet. The one on the rock. The banshee was washing the lead biker's leathers. It was a warning that you of all people should NOT pick that helmet," Kelly said.

"Why not?" Nareen and Carl asked.

Kelly heaved a sigh. "Because she is you, Nareen."

"What do you mean?" Nareen asked.

"Well, you know how Carl's rider was another me?" She waited until Nareen nodded. "Well, the lead biker is another you. I saw her face when she was catching us on the staircase. The banshee was warning you!"

Nareen looked down, wondering why she hadn't worked that out. Especially since the motorbike rider's note had said they'd changed the bikers' lives twice already. The first was Carl letting them out and the second was when Kelly had not let her choose the lead rider's helmet. By heeding the banshee's warning, they had changed the course of events. In doing so, they'd saved the lead biker's life and her own life as well.

She was about to apologise to Kelly when Carl slapped himself on the forehead. "That's it!" he blurted.

Neither girl spoke.

"Duh!" Carl said. "They kept talking about a passage out. You know, that guy with the microphone. Well this," he said, stabbing a finger at the shield, "is it."

Nareen opened her mouth to protest, but he swept on, talking faster and faster. "The banshee — she granted me an answer to a question. I didn't tell you before because her answer didn't make sense. But it does now! I asked how we could get out of here and she said we have to 'rearrange the letters.'"

Still, neither girl spoke. "Rearrange the letters,"

he said impatiently. "These letters — *An energetic world leader remains*." He turned to Kelly. "You're the Scrabble champ. Here, you do it."

"It's, um, not that easy," said Kelly slowly. "You know, I usually just fiddle around with the letters . . . "

"Yeah," interrupted Carl, "but you sorted out *Signpost huge hole* with no letters."

"But hang on," Kelly said. "I was just comparing the two. *Signpost huge hole* and *Nugget shoe polish*. I was looking for a pattern. You know — how they related to each other. It's easy when you have both. But I don't even know where to start on this."

Nareen put down her pack and began to rummage around. At last she fished out a packet of pasta and handed it to Kelly. "Would this help? It's alphabet pasta. You could use the letters like Scrabble tiles."

Kelly looked unsure but took the packet.

"If I'm right," said Carl, "then this will be a dead-end corridor. I'll go check it out while you start on that." Before anyone could answer, he sped off down the corridor.

In less than a minute, he was dashing past them again. "Dead end that-a-way," he yelled.

Soon he was back once more, puffing so hard he couldn't talk. Finally he resorted to the compère's throat-slitting gesture and pointed back the way he'd come.

"So it *is* a dead end," Kelly said.

"And the door into the stadium locked behind us," Nareen said.

Not content to take her word for it, Carl swung on the handle.

Sure enough, it was locked.

Recoil and Rewind

Kelly took off her pack and sat down propped up against it. Nareen joined her and they sorted out the letters they needed on the ground in front of them. Nareen put the spare ones back in the packet, but Kelly made no move to start shuffling the letters.

"Well?" asked Carl. He'd given her the answer but all she did was stare from the pile of pasta letters to the plaque and back again.

"I don't know where to start," she said.

"Maybe we have to perform an exit version of the incantation that opened the chrysalis in the first place," suggested Nareen.

"But shorter," Carl said. He couldn't remember the original incantation, but he did remember that, as he stood behind the tree, it seemed to take forever to get to the only line he knew — the last line. "Uncoil and unwind," he murmured to himself. To think that was what got them into this in the first place. Not that it was his fault. Nareen was always going to open it anyway. Dad had told her often enough not to muck around with things she didn't understand, but Nareen still had to go and meddle.

"We can't do *uncoil and unwind*," Kelly said, "but . . . " She shuffled a few letters around, then shook her head and tapped her nose. "We can do *recoil and rewind*."

"Sounds good," Nareen said. "And it makes sense, too."

As the girls muttered to themselves, Carl went digging in the packs to see if he could find any food. There were three pots of peaches in syrup and a bar of chocolate. He pocketed the chocolate and handed out the fruit.

Kelly stared off into the distance as she ate her fruit. Carl had expected her to be shuffling and rearranging, not just staring into space. When he couldn't stand it any more, he fished out his pen and handed it to Nareen. "Write down the incantation. You know, the one that opened it."

Nareen smoothed out the cardboard packaging from around the fruit pots and wrote:

Fire of sapphire
stairway of time
hidden and creased
I grant you release
stairway sublime
uncoil and unwind.

Kelly shook her head. "We can't do *stairway* or *sublime* but . . . " She trailed off. Then slowly, too slowly for Carl's liking, she began sifting the letters. "We can do . . . yes . . . " She sat back and pointed down. Next to *recoil* and *rewind* she'd placed the word *release*.

"And," said Nareen, leaning forwards and shuffling letters, "we can do *grant*."

"Leaving *me*," Carl finished off. "That's it. Grant me . . ."

Nareen whacked her hand over his mouth. "Don't say it," she hissed. "We have to be sure. It's not only us who are stranded here. The bikers you let out are stranded here as well. They're relying on us to get them back where they belong. If it is right, we three all have to say it together."

"Unless," said Kelly, raising an eyebrow at him, "you're planning on only saving yourself and leaving the rest of us behind."

"Of course I'm not. What do you think I am?" Carl asked. The girls exchanged glances. How he hated it when girls did that.

Kelly leaned forward and rearranged the words so the pasta read:

Grant me release recoil and rewind.

"What do you think?" she asked. "Is that the answer?"

"It has to be," said Carl, leaping to his feet. "What else could it be? It makes sense."

Nareen nodded. "I can't see how it could be anything else. It matches everything: the incantation, what the banshee told Carl and what the compère said about earning safe passage out for him and his friends. But what if we're wrong? What if we let something else out? This is a locked corridor. We've got nowhere to run if we do."

Kelly bit her lip. "I don't even want to think about it," she muttered.

"But we have to," Nareen said. "It's not just us on the line. And what if turning ghost changes things? What if that makes it not work? What if you can't even be part-ghost for it to work? And, besides, do you believe the compère?"

"No, but banshees aren't bad spirits," Kelly said. "Even if we can't believe anyone else here — the butler or the compère — we can believe her. I mean, she appeared because of your ancestors being Scottish. She's not part of this place. We have to believe her."

Nareen ran a hand through her hair, frowning. She managed a small nod, but still did nothing.

Carl took a deep breath. Why, oh why, did girls have to agonise over the obvious? The answer was right in front of their eyes. All they had to do was say it, not talk about it. Not look for any other solutions. Just say it. It was time he took charge. He grabbed a strap of each pack. "I'll beat three with my foot. We'll start after three and all say one word per beat."

Still looking worried, Kelly and Nareen took hold of a strap of each pack. Then, at the third beat of Carl's foot, they chanted in unison with his stamping, "Grant me release, recoil and rewind."

The moment they had articulated the final "d" of "rewind", the corridor began to spin, faster and faster and faster. It twisted and heaved, tipping Carl and the contents of the pack, which he'd forgotten to close, up and over and over. He tumbled head over heels amid a tornado of Monopoly money, counters, pasta letters, raincoats and shoe polish. A Community Chest card hit him in the face. For a split second, he saw he'd won second prize in a beauty contest before it was whipped away again. He couldn't see Kelly or Nareen. He opened his mouth to yell to them and swallowed a mouthful of soap. He spat it out and was hit from behind by something a lot heavier.

The next thing he was aware of was the sound of birdsong. Nah, Carl thought, that can't be right. Something was tickling his nostrils. It smelled like grass. He raised his head and opened his eyes. It *was* grass. He rolled over and sat up. He was at the top of the property, between the fence and the last of the family's trees. There was no sign of the spiral staircase and he wasn't floating. He was sitting on the grass. Better still, he was no longer transparent. Kelly and Nareen were lying face down just out of reach. He leapt to his feet but, before he could dash over to see if they were all right, Kelly raised her head and Nareen propped herself up. "Did it work?" she asked.

Kelly sat up and then looked down at herself. "My T-shirt. Look, Nareen, look!" she squealed.

Carl couldn't believe his ears. He'd saved them and all Kelly noticed was that some T-shirt her mother had bought her wasn't ruined. Neither of them had noticed that the packs were nowhere to be seen.

"None of us is transparent either," said Nareen, grabbing Kelly's arm. "We're out!"

She started laughing, dancing around and around like Gran used to when she went a bit weird. Carl couldn't help but laugh. It was as if everything had gone back to the way it was when they first opened the chrysalis. He stuck his hand in his pocket to check his theory. Yep, the chocolate was gone. In its place was a printout of the Nürburgring racetrack and, in the other pocket, his mobile, earplugs for his mobile, his biro, USB pen drive and back door key. He checked his watch. The second hand was ticking. It was working again and reckoned that the time was twenty-eight minutes past twelve.

"Looks like we're right back where we started before you opened the chrysalis. An hour and a bit after lunch," he said. Kelly beamed at him. She glanced over her shoulder at Nareen, then took a step towards him.

Speaking so quietly Carl could barely hear her, she said, "Thanks, Carl. You were pretty cool in there . . . I mean . . . it's just we couldn't have got out without you and . . . " she trailed off, looking down at her T-shirt. "I know I went a bit crazy in there ... it's just, um, I never get to shop like that. We can only afford something like one new T-shirt every six months and this is it. My mum would have killed me if I'd wrecked it on the first day I wore it."

For the first time in his life Carl couldn't think of anything to say. By time his brain understood that Kelly had actually told him that she thought he was cool, the girls were already heading down through the trees, chattering wildly. Kelly was going on about how her mother wouldn't even have known they'd gone anywhere. Everything was as it was before Nareen had found the chrysalis, and the bikers would also be back where they belonged.

Carl was about to follow them down to the house when a thought struck him. He waited until he was sure the girls could no longer see him and, keeping an ear out to make sure their voices kept receding, he climbed back up towards the fence. It took him more than ten minutes to find what he was looking for. But there it was — just as Nareen had found it. A harmless looking chrysalis shaped like a spiral. Intact and swinging on a blade of grass. Waiting for him.

Carl took a quick look around to make sure the coast was clear. It was. He rolled the printout of the Nürburgring racetrack into a cone. Then, as gently as he could, he picked the piece of grass. Taking great care not to jolt or damage it, he slid the chrysalis inside the paper cone. As he carried it down towards the house he told himself that Nareen was bound to have the incantation written down. He would search her room. No doubt she'd have a whole lot of other stuff about the chrysalis stashed in there as well.

One day he was going to go to a Formula One race at the Nürburgring in Germany.

One day — soon.